Raising Empowered Learners

Raising Empowered Learners

Cultivating Students' Curiosity, Character, and Confidence

Ed Madison

ROWMAN & LITTLEFIELD
Lanham • Boulder • New York • London

Published by Rowman & Littlefield
An imprint of The Rowman & Littlefield Publishing Group, Inc.
4501 Forbes Boulevard, Suite 200, Lanham, Maryland 20706
www.rowman.com

86-90 Paul Street, London EC2A 4NE, United Kingdom

Copyright © 2024 by Ed Madison

All rights reserved. No part of this book may be reproduced in any form or by any electronic or mechanical means, including information storage and retrieval systems, without written permission from the publisher, except by a reviewer who may quote passages in a review.

British Library Cataloguing in Publication Information Available

Library of Congress Cataloging-in-Publication Data

Names: Madison, Ed, 1958– author.
Title: Raising empowered learners : cultivating students' curiosity, character, and confidence / Ed Madison.
Description: Lanham Maryland : Rowman & Littlefield Publishing Group, 2024. | Includes bibliographical references. | Summary: "Raising Empowered Learners gives actionable tools rooted in journalistic strategies that help educators and parents inspire students to excel and develop resiliency as we emerge into a post-COVID world"—Provided by publisher.
Identifiers: LCCN 2023035839 (print) | LCCN 2023035840 (ebook) | ISBN 9781475869668 (cloth) | ISBN 9781475869675 (paperback) | ISBN 9781475869682 (epub)
Subjects: LCSH: Motivation in education. | Motivation (Psychology) in children. | Resilience (Personality trait) in children.
Classification: LCC LB1065 .M2743 2024 (print) | LCC LB1065 (ebook) | DDC 370.15/4—dc23/eng/20230912
LC record available at https://lccn.loc.gov/2023035839
LC ebook record available at https://lccn.loc.gov/2023035840

*To my parents, Eddie and Davetta Madison,
who were my first teachers.*

Contents

Foreword	ix
Preface	xiii
Acknowledgments	xv
Chapter 1: Ending the Blame Game	1
Chapter 2: The Myth of the Reluctant Learner	9
Chapter 3: Kids Don't Need Fixing	17
Chapter 4: Flipping the Switch	37
Chapter 5: The Confidence Conundrum	53
Chapter 6: Voice and Choice	63
Chapter 7: Amplification	69
Chapter 8: Advocating for Children with Special Needs	79
Chapter 9: Your Child's First Teacher	87
Chapter 10: Call to Action	93
Appendix: List of Parent Advocacy Resources	99

Foreword

Education is not preparation for life, it is life itself.

—John Dewey

What kind of education do we want for our children? Although this can be a hotly debated question, most people agree that a key goal of education is to prepare children for the future. The challenge is that the future is unknowable. And, to further complicate the matter, there is not just one singular future but multiple, possible futures. So how can parents help educate students for an unknowable future? This question highlights a challenge that I've called the *Education for Unknowable Futures* paradox.

The paradox has, of course, not stopped schools in their efforts to educate young people. That said, it does offer pause to those of us who are parents. If we stop to think about it, we will soon realize that schools tend to prepare young people for a somewhat narrow view of the future: the *likely future*. Indeed, schools tend to focus on teaching students what is already known and doable in the hopes that what is taught now will still have some value in the foreseeable future.

In this way, school represents a promissory note. If you learn this now, then someday it will be beneficial to your future. Although most of us can agree that there are various things taught in school that likely will be needed in the foreseeable future, for example, knowing how to read and write. We can also agree that for so many generations of students and their families this promissory note has failed to live up to its promise. This book thereby calls us to go beyond this transactional relationship with learning and toward a more transformative approach aimed at empowering children to make the world a better place for themselves and others. It also calls us to have the courage to reimagine and do our part in helping our children realize their full potential in and outside of this place called school.

Indeed, education is about the possible. And, as parents, we want so much more for our children. Yes, we want them to be able to be skilled and productive members of society, but we also want to empower them to be able to shape their own futures. Why stop then at educating them for likely futures? Why limit the full horizon of what is possible when educating our children?

We must always remember that as parents we are also teachers. We are our children's first teachers. And we play a nontrivial role in helping to inspire them about what can be learned from life itself, including the setbacks along the way. We can and, in fact, *must* instill in them hope for much brighter futures. We can help empower them to go beyond "what is" and imagine "what can" and "should be."

This book offers ideas, strategies, and examples to help equip our children to be self-determined learners now and into the future. It is about advocating for so much more when it comes to our children's education and, most importantly, it is about empowering them to exercise their own creative agency. Doing so will equip them to step confidently into current and future uncertainties, unleash their imagination, and put their learning to work to make the world a better place for themselves and others.

Our children are natural learners, they want to know, they want to act, they want to fulfill their full potential as future makers. Don't we then owe it our own children—and all children—the opportunities and support they need to realize this potential? Our children are ready. But they need us. They need our persistent support and belief in them to become the self-determined makers of their own futures. Admittedly, this is not always easy. And we will sometimes make mistakes, but we must persist. We can show them, by our own actions, how to learn from setbacks, how to develop an unshakeable sense of the possible, and how to be a positive force in the world. We can also advocate for them. And this book offers insights for how we can fulfill our responsibility as parents to help educate our children for the broadest and brightest of possible futures. The time is now to expand our understanding of such empowering ideas and, most importantly, put them into action.

Ronald A. Beghetto
Pinnacle West Presidential Chair and Professor
Arizona State University

Preface

Parents and teachers seek the best educational experiences for their children, despite structural obstacles and economic disparities that can make our public education system anything but equitable. Some begrudgingly believe there is little they can do to effect real change. Others learn to "work the system," insisting that the children they are entrusted with raising do not become victims of antiquated policies and practices that don't serve their best interests.

Attending less-than-optimal schools can negatively impact all students' prospects. However, students of color are particularly vulnerable when their educational experience fails to connect or seems relevant culturally. Rather than thrive and fulfill their highest potential, they risk becoming statistics caught in so-called "achievement gaps" or worse.

Brown v. the Board of Education was a landmark 1954 Supreme Court decision intending to outlaw "separate but equal" school segregation laws in southern states. Yet, 70 years later, many of our public schools remain segregated and are far from equal. Despite best intentions, the more we endeavor to "reform education," the more frustrated we become about how it remains the same.

Most students carry smartphones capable of providing instant answers to nearly any question they may care to ask. Artificial intelligence takes the technological revolution two steps further, providing pages of responses that marvel most imaginations. Yet, rather than embrace these technologies, they are ignored or forbidden in many school districts. Students are the first to sense the disconnect. Some tune out, and far too many drop out.

This book is for parents and educators who are fed up with business as usual. It provides tangible strategies for how teachers, administrators, and parents can form meaningful alliances that support young people in fulfilling their promises.

Through these pages, you'll meet teachers who are also parents and discover how they've had to maneuver to ensure their children aren't "left behind." More importantly, you'll discover how many have empowered their children to advocate for themselves. When students are curious and confident, it builds character. They develop resilience, led by an internal compass that points them in a positive direction without fail. They also are less likely to fall prey to mental health problems linked to social media shaming and bullying.

We all want schools that properly prepare youth to thrive and have fulfilling futures. Superman is not coming to intervene, and there is no "magic wand" that, once waived, will miraculously "fix" our education system. However, within these pages, you'll discover a way forward. By understanding your rights and advocating for your family's educational needs, you and your child will prevail.

Acknowledgments

I offer special thanks to my family for their inspiration and support. I'm grateful to Esther Wojcicki, whose teaching legacy informs many ideas. Also, our Journalistic Learning Initiative board of directors, including Esther Wojcicki, Ritch Colbert, Berk Nelson, Susan Costillo, Amira Barger, Suzzette Martinez-Malavet, and Hank Stern. Special thanks to Hans Boyle, JLI's super talented researcher and grant writer. Also, the JLI team, which works tirelessly to enrich the lives of the students we serve. Specifically, they include Glenda Gordon, Melissa Wantz, Rachel Guldin, Bo Brusco, Maya Lazaro, Jael Calloway, Auna Colipano, Hailey O'Donnell, Emani Powell, Noeme Teofilo, and Clarence Kim. Additionally, I wish to thank our University of Oregon School of Journalism and Communication dean, Juan-Carlos Molleda. My academic mentors are Ron Beghetto, Rene Hobbs, Jerry Rosiek, Leslie Steeves, and Tim Gleason. And our thought partners, Ross Anderson, Matt Coleman, and Tracy Bousselot. Finally, I thank our generous supporters, Nancy and Dave Petrone, the Roundhouse Foundation, the Meyer Memorial Trust, the Scripps Family Impact Fund, and the NewSchools Venture Fund.

Chapter 1

Ending the Blame Game

The "blame game" is ever-apparent in public education. Decades of unfulfilled hopes and failed policies lead parents to fault teachers, teachers to fault administrators and policymakers, and students to try and make sense of it all.

Nothing in this book intends to dishonor or denigrate the hard work of dedicated teachers. We often blame educators for the failings of misguided policies administrators force them to follow. Well-meaning administrators are often caught in the middle. Underappreciated, underpaid, and overworked, 16% of teachers changed schools or leave the profession annually (National Center for Education Statistics, 2015).

We are also losing teachers exhausted from defending against relentless attacks on their profession. Corporate and conservative-backed groups are challenging teachers' freedom to determine course content. The result is legislation that seeks to ban certain books and prohibit discussing race, ethnicity, gender, and social justice themes. Regardless of where you weigh in on these debates, it is fair to say that caring parents will always be passionate about how their children are educated.

This book aims to rise above the heated and often unconstructive rhetoric of the moment and provide parents and teachers with practical strategies for supporting children's growth and development. It focuses on how administrators, teachers, and parents can join forces to improve systems that no longer serve our youth.

The COVID-19 pandemic exacerbated teacher burnout. "We're going to lose an entire generation of not only students but teachers," education scholar Shea Martin told the *New York Times* in November 2020 (Singer, 2020). Twenty-eight percent of educators polled by the nation's most prominent teachers' union said the coronavirus made them more likely to retire early. While vaccines may have abated the worst stages of the pandemic, COVID forever impacted a generation of learners in ways social science is still attempting to discern.

No one enters teaching for the paycheck. More frequently, becoming an educator is a calling to make a difference in preparing students to meet the challenges ahead. This authentic calling led me to pivot from a successful full-time career as a media producer and enter academia to research student motivation and explore new possibilities for improving education.

My mom taught grade school, and my dad was a journalist, so interest in the intersection of these disciplines is likely a part of my DNA. There were always two teachers in my life at any given time—the one at school and the second one at home. Rides anywhere were opportunities for my mom to drill me on multiplication tables, and I had better be prepared. To this day, despite having earned a PhD, I'm not overly embarrassed to admit I shudder at the thought of instantly recalling an accurate answer for seven times eight.

While I sometimes resented the uninvited tutoring, I later realized my mother had only the best intentions. My parents were products of the post-depression era South—still very much affected by Jim Crow laws that sought to limit Black Americans' educational opportunities. They were committed to not having their offspring traumatized or held back in ways their parents and they knew too well.

Having a mother who understood how to navigate educational systems from the inside afforded me great privileges unavailable to many of my peers. Often, to my embarrassment, she made demands of my teachers; and, more importantly, taught me to follow her example. "Remember who you are," was a familiar phrase in our household. "We are Madisons."

Later in life, I learned untold stories about our family's heritage. I was born in Tulsa, Oklahoma, as was my father. My mom was born in Muskogee, fifty miles south. Her side of the family were descendants of a long line of Baptist ministers. A well-kept secret was that my great-grandfather's church was torched during the 1921 Tulsa Race Massacre—among the many atrocities. Like much of America, I had never heard about this act of brutality until later in life. My parents sought to spare my two siblings and me from the burden of brutality that had haunted their generation. With that lineage, you can imagine they were hyper-vigilant about equity, social justice, and ensuring their children's dignity.

During my grandparents' era, people of color were conditioned to be subservient, stay in their place, and not make waves. However, by the 1960s, much of Black America rejected that stance. If an authority figure was out-of-line or mistreated me, my mother wanted to know. "Stand up for yourself and look them in the eye," she would say.

Summoning the courage to push back is no easy feat for many Black, indigenous, and people of color. One must become self-determined and willing to stand up for what is right. Modern-era Black women are often acknowledged for their inner strength. Harriet Tubman, Rosa Parks, Maya Angelou, Oprah Winfrey, Viola Davis, and the heroic characters they portray immediately come to mind. Always poised and elegant, former first lady Michelle Obama models bravery and resolve. She rejected tropes that she was an "angry black woman" for speaking her mind about social injustices.

Other colonized and subjugated populations also struggle with overcoming learned passivity. Several of my Asian university students tell me they are taught never to look a professor in the eye. Similarly, a false sense of hierarchy has conditioned many Latinx parents and students to be submissive in the presence of "authority figures." Such challenges are not limited to race and ethnicity. Class struggles cut across cultural boundaries. In her Pulitzer Prize–winning book, *Caste: The Origins of Our Discontent*, author Isabel Wilkerson argues that social stratification, whether explicit or implicit, informs how we relate as societies and make sense of the world (Wilkerson, 2023).

Gender conditioning can lead girls to diminish their power. In 2015, Dove's #LikeAGirl viral video campaign proved this point. When asked, "Show me what it looks like to run like a girl," male and female respondents would prance, wave their hair, and make small gestures–-in stark contrast to demonstrating signs of strength.

But those days are numbered. Women and people of color are shattering glass ceilings, emerging as corporate and political leaders, and becoming strong role models. Whether you are a parent, teacher, or administrator, you must muster the courage to respectfully advocate for the young people you are entrusted with raising and educating. Simultaneously, you must teach them to do the same. The "squeaky wheel" gathers traction and fulfills its intent. The world is more competitive than ever, and timidness is rarely rewarded.

Advocacy and activism benefit from a range of foot soldiers employing differing tactics yet sharing the same aims. The civil rights movement needed Dr. King, Thurgood Marshall, and Malcolm X—and Ida B. Wells, decades before—to advance social justice. In the battle for educational justice, I'm inspired by the work of Dr. Bettina Love, who advocates for immediate, organized, and strategic action to "dismantle oppressive structures while creating more liberatory practices" (Abolitionist Teaching Network, n.d.).

You may prefer a more measured approach. However, it is crucial to recognize that all forms of deliberate action can make a significant difference. Mustering the courage to speak up and teaching our children to speak for themselves is imperative. And, you don't have to go it alone. Banding together with like-minded parents, teachers, and allies fortifies strength. Knowledge is power, and this book is designed to empower you to understand and oppose deeply rooted forces in institutionalized education that no longer serve our children.

FOUNDATIONS

In 2016, we formalized the work of the Journalistic Learning Initiative (JLI), a 501(c)(3) nonprofit organization whose mission is to empower students to discover their voice and improve academic outcomes, and engage in self-directed learning through project-based storytelling.

Central to our work is having students discover that they have a voice and that their voices matter and can make a difference in their communities and the world. Telling stories is how we make sense of the world and share our truths.

JLI simultaneously endeavors to cultivate students' curiosity, confidence, and character. Curiosity means rekindling a sense of wonder about the world and one's desire to explore future possibilities. Confidence is boldness or self-assurance in one's abilities. Finally, character gives young people a foundation and compass to navigate the world. Rather than seek external validation of their worthiness, students emerge as inner-directed and resilient. When we focus on helping students develop curiosity, confidence, and character, academics improve as a natural outcome.

We call this approach *journalistic learning*. The methods are rooted in professional journalism practices and are beneficial because they honor and build upon students' intrinsic interests—the wealth of topics and ideas they already possess. Of course, they benefit from exploring topics beyond their current experiences—but we find students are more responsive when you first meet them where they are.

Education thought leader Esther Wojcicki's work informs our approach. She led Palo Alto High School's acclaimed journalism program to serve more than 800 students annually. Recently retired from the classroom, Esther continues to do TED Talks, present at conferences, and advocate internationally for journalistic learning reforms. She's the author of a best-selling book on a topic she knows quite a bit about—*How to Raise Successful People*, which reveals how she successfully raised three outstanding daughters. Anne Wojcicki is the founder and CEO of Twenty-three and Me, the successful DNA testing and analysis company; Susan Wojcicki is the former CEO of YouTube; and Janet Wojcicki is a renowned anthropologist and epidemiologist.

I first met Esther in 2010 while a graduate student searching for a dissertation topic. We shared a panel at a Stanford University journalism conference, where she arrived with three of her high school students in tow. Their poise and professionalism immediately impressed me. Of course, Palo Alto is among the wealthiest communities in America, and the high school is situated directly across from Stanford. Facebook and Google are nearby.

The encounter led me to study Paly (as locals know it) and its journalism program for 2 years and video record teacher-student interactions. I was curious whether the academic proficiency and self-reflective confidence I witnessed were an anomaly. Or could we possibly replicate the program's instructional strategies in far less affluent communities?

I first published my findings in my dissertation and later in *Newsworthy: Cultivating Critical Thinkers, Readers, and Writers in Language Arts Classrooms* through Teachers College Press at Columbia University.

It turns out, what most journalists intuitively know and practice dramatically benefits students. Much like in a newsroom, students become more intently invested and thrive when collaborating on projects they initiate.

Esther and I formed a nonprofit organization that became the Journalistic Learning Initiative, with support from philanthropist Tara Guber. In its first 8 years, JLI has served nearly 7,500 students at over 75 middle and high schools in Oregon, Idaho, Washington, Arizona, and California. More recently, through generous benefactors, foundation grants, and corporate partnerships, we have launched programs accessible to students and teachers nationwide.

Throughout this book, I'll describe JLI's principles and strategies and discuss how your child or students can best use them to achieve greater academic success and, perhaps more importantly, a stronger sense of self and their place in the world. Education policy often overly focuses on teaching future-based skills without considering a child's present need to feel grounded, nurtured, and confident. As you read these pages, please note that I've used pseudonyms to protect their privacy when referencing minors and specific individuals.

KEY TAKEAWAYS

This chapter argued for ending the "blame game," which pits parents against teachers and administrators. Rather, there are constructive and collaborative ways to engage with one another that support student growth and development.

It also offered foundational information about the Journalistic Learning Initiative, and its mission to transform student experiences through honoring and tapping young peoples' intrinsic interests. JLI's work is informed by strategies developed at Palo Alto High School in Northern California.

QUESTIONS TO CONSIDER

- Think back to your own middle and high school experience. Were your interests honored? How did it impact your feelings about school?

- Whether you're a parent or an educator, how might you begin to honor the interests of the young people in your life?
- How might that make a difference in your relationships?

REFERENCES

Abolitionist Teaching Network. (n.d.). *Activists in residence*. Abolitionist Teaching Network. Retrieved March 29, 2023, from https://abolitionistteachingnetwork.org/activists-in-residenc

National Center for Education Statistics. (2015). *Teacher Turnover: Stayers, Movers, and Leavers*. nces.ed.gov. Retrieved March 25, 2023, from https://nces.ed.gov/programs/coe/indicator/slc/teacher-turnover

Singer, N. (2020, November 30). *Teaching in the pandemic: "This is not sustainable."* The New York Times. Retrieved March 25, 2023, from https://www.nytimes.com/2020/11/30/us/teachers-remote-learning-burnout.html

Wilkerson, I. (2023). *Caste*. Penguin.

Chapter 2

The Myth of the Reluctant Learner

"Your son looks like a pretty unmotivated kiddo to me."

An assistant principal at our son's middle school uttered those words during a second round of parent-teacher conferences. He was labeled a reluctant learner at age 12.

How can a child or student ever have an opportunity to thrive with that characterization ascribed to their potential? Deficit narratives such as these can get passed around between administrators and faculty, haunting a child through their entire grade school experience.

Rather than cause a scene, I held back from speaking my mind. "How dare you," and a few expletives were the words I wanted to shout out. But I kept my composure and suppressed my anger.

If you are reading this book, you are likely a parent or guardian frustrated by report card grades and test scores that don't reflect the potential you see in your child and are unsure about what to do next. Conversely, you may be a teacher discouraged from having to follow failed policies you instinctively know don't serve your students.

In either case, you are among millions who may feel disempowered by systemic forces that impede students' innate yearning to learn.

"You see the difference between sixth and eighth grade," says Melissa Wantz. She taught middle and high school English and journalism for 20 years in Southern California before retiring in Oregon and leading the Journalistic Learning Initiative's instructional design and educator fellowship programs. "The sense of innocence and wonder you see in sixth-graders is slowly replaced by a questioning of authority, peer pressures, and a somewhat jaded perspective about school."

Think about it. Even with larger classes, elementary school teachers spend all day and a full year with their students. An educator may teach five or six sections of their designated discipline by middle school. The personal connection that benefits the elementary experience is lost, and it becomes easier for students to hide out and fall behind.

By middle school, students become innately aware they are measured and compared to their peers. Ricky realizes his buddy Jordan is in a higher-achieving reading group. Desiree discovers she is repeating math assignments from the previous year while her friends are moving on. These revelations can be jolting for a young person trying to cultivate a stronger sense of self.

Consequently, middle school is where many students begin to solidify a rigid sense of their abilities. "I'm not creative" or "I can't write" are common sentiments, and by eighth grade, they often have collected evidence that supports these beliefs.

Stanford researcher Carol Dweck's fixed versus *growth mindset* work has achieved currency in education circles for accurately articulating this phenomenon. Fixed beliefs confine one's ability to act and develop new skills. Dweck argues that students can begin to break these rigid thought systems by first acknowledging they are mere beliefs and questioning their validity. Experiencing anxiety when facing a blank page doesn't condemn one to be a poor writer. What comes easy for some students take others more time.

Teachers also have the power to disrupt rather than reinforce these negative beliefs. French philosopher and activist, Michel Foucault, whose work on power and social change remains highly influential in academia, argued authority figures like teachers can unintentionally conjure these identities like "poor writer" or "reluctant learner" into existence through linguistic categorizing and labeling.

Noncompliance is a typical behavior met with a referral slip and a trip to the principal's office. "He won't open his textbook and follow along with the other students," is a common complaint. Teachers and administrators often misread such behavior as defiance when it may actually be an indicator of less obvious concerns.

University of Oregon researcher Rhonda Nese studies disparities in school disciplinary practices that often result in students of color being labeled and punished far more often than their peers. "We know from research that the school-to-prison pipeline is a very real thing. Students who receive harsh and disproportionate exclusionary discipline are much more likely to drop out of school, have an academic failure, end up incarcerated, end up using substances, and suicide rates go up," Nese says.

In the world of education, this means teachers or administrators singling out nonconforming students as "deviants" or "troublemakers." However, these "troublemakers" may, in fact, be students struggling with learning disabilities, financial troubles at home or other personal issues unknown to their teacher.

Again, the intention here is not to denigrate educators. Hard-working teachers across the country strive every day to inspire and engage their students. They deserve our respect and admiration. Unfortunately, many educators are forced to follow flawed policies they instinctively know aren't benefiting their students.

In the often chaotic middle school environment, when one English teacher is cycling through ninety-plus sixth graders daily, it becomes much harder to forge connections with each student. That's why it's essential to remember labels are more than just descriptions.

Natalie Hollabaugh left the teaching profession to become a defense attorney who supports juvenile justice reform. She could no longer reconcile the disconnect between what she intuitively felt was best for students and the adverse effect of harsh disciplinary policies prevalent in schools. "I pretty quickly realized that the school-to-prison pipeline was very obvious. In my role as a teacher, I was required essentially to perpetuate it and perpetuate that harm," Hollabaugh says. "I realized pretty quickly that I couldn't do my job as I was being expected to do by administrators while simultaneously not perpetuating that harm. I got really frustrated and realized it was kind of like where the rubber meets the road, and I couldn't do that anymore."

Students who hear "troublemaker" or "poor writer" take it to heart. Soon the label becomes a self-fulfilling prophecy. Lucy, afraid of hearing comments like "slow reader," shuns reading aloud in class. Cameron, worried about his writing capabilities, begins procrastinating on his writing assignments and then avoids them altogether.

Labels like "reluctant learner," while damaging, are also shortsighted and don't tell a complete story. Numerous highly accomplished individuals were labeled "slow learners" or were thought to have limited potential.

The grade school writing of Agatha Christie, one of the world's most acclaimed mystery authors, was considered illegible. Doctors later diagnosed her as suffering from dysgraphia, a learning disorder that negatively affects penmanship, spelling, and math skills. Christie had no trouble reading or conceiving grand plot lines. She cultivated an ability to juggle many story lines simultaneously, committing seemingly random ideas to paper in up to six notebooks. Rather than formalizing her stories through conventional writing, Christie turned to dictating her mysteries and romance novels. Imagine the literary world's loss if she had allowed her disability to derail her creative spirit. Christie authored more than 75 books, making her among the most prolific writers in her genre (Masters in Special Education Program Guide, 2021).

Richard Branson, the billionaire behind the multinational Virgin Group and former President Obama's occasional kitesurfing partner, was once told by the headmaster of his boarding school that he would either end up a millionaire or in prison.

Early in his life, Branson struggled with dyslexia, a learning disorder affecting his reading ability, and said he was "the dumbest person at school." Branson decided to drop out and start his own magazine.

Branson's *Student*, a youth-culture publication run by students out of his cofounder's parents' basement, offered ideas he deemed "too revolutionary to be aired in the school magazine." The magazine covered topics that mattered to him, like music and the Vietnam war, with the first edition selling $8,000 in advertising. Branson would go on to start a small mail-order record company called Virgin to support the publication, eventually expanding that venture into a record shop and then finally creating his own recording label—Virgin Records.

Now, all of this is not to say if teachers avoid shortsighted labels, their students will wind up with wildly successful careers. Not everyone has the innate sense for riveting narratives like Agatha Christie or the business savvy of Richard Branson. And indeed, a good amount of luck helped both realize their dreams. However, like many other students, Branson and Christie had passions that their teachers initially discounted through discouraging labels.

Passion, after all, is what educators should strive to ignite in their students. Young people should come to school unafraid of labels, eager to learn, and ready to challenge themselves. It's the kind of classroom environment parents want for their children.

However, the roots of today's classroom remain rooted in the Industrial Revolution. Public education has not reflected the era's technological innovations. School administrators began implementing policies to prepare children for the workforce rather than cultivate a passion for learning.

As the nation saw its cities bustle with economic activity and population surges, education administrators looked to factories as models for organizing and teaching increasingly large class sizes. Standardization accelerated, with grading becoming more common and schools emphasizing uniformity. Educational reformers debated the best ways to teach America's children throughout the nineteenth and twentieth centuries, with progressive thinkers arguing for more student-centered approaches. Yet, the classroom as we know it today hasn't evolved much since industrialization.

Most students still walk into a four-walled classroom, with rows of desks facing toward a sole instructor. They take their seats and act as passive receptors of information, providing input only when they raise their hand and are called upon to give the "correct answer" to a question. Many watch the clock above their teacher, waiting for the school bell to ring, deliver them from the doldrums of traditional instruction, and send them off for more of the same.

Of course, teachers' leeway in adapting their curriculums and the resources they have to carry them out depends mainly on the federally and state-funded and state-run public school system. Affluent communities tend to have a more extensive tax base, affording them greater leeway. Those funds usually come with requirements that teachers get their students to meet specific benchmarks.

The system isn't working. In 2021, Gallup found that only 28% of parents were completely or somewhat satisfied with their child's K through 12 education. The same survey found 55% of parents were entirely or partly dissatisfied. Gallup began tracking that question back in 1999, and since then, only roughly one in 10 U.S. parents have reported being completely satisfied (Brenan, 2021).

So how can we, parents and teachers, spark that desire to learn within our students? How can we protect their passion for learning as they go through an education system that often discourages their curiosity and interests?

The rest of this book will endeavor to answer these questions and help you apply the practices we've learned through the Journalistic Learning Initiative's years of working with countless students and teachers. However, the answer to all these questions is common sense: at the most basic level, we need to allow students to find motivation from within, and science proves this.

Much of the research underpinning this book relates to *self-determination theory*, which psychology researchers Edward Deci and Richard Ryan first thoroughly articulated in the mid-eighties. One of social psychology's most cited frameworks, self-determination theory, argues that humans are shaped by fundamental psychological needs and not solely by outside forces (Deci & Ryan, 2014). Put another way, we aren't solely motivated by rewards or deterred by fear of punishment. We have innate desires and ambitions, as well as a drive for growth, intellectual and psychological.

The power of self-motivation has certainly not been overlooked in the private sector. Author and former speechwriter for Vice President Al Gore, Daniel Pink, wrote about the effectiveness of encouraging self-motivation in the business world in his 2011 book *Drive*.

Pink argued extrinsic motivators like money and reprimands, perhaps counterintuitively, depressed workers' engagement, turning potentially exciting tasks into . . . well, work. Pink instead asserted the carrot-and-stick rewards system used by many corporations paled in comparison to tapping into workers' *intrinsic* motivation—their desire to be self-directed, to learn new skills, and to work on something meaningful (Pink, 2011).

Pink drew his observations from Deci and Ryan's research. According to self-determination theory, intrinsic motivation lies on the highest level of the motivation spectrum, and there are three components needed to attain it: autonomy, competence, and relatedness.

Autonomy simply refers to one's sense that their actions are self-directed, while competence refers to one's sense of being capable of performing a task, that one can meet a challenge and accomplish a goal. Finally, relatedness refers to one's sense of belonging and support. Think of autonomy, competence, and relatedness as three legs of a tripod. If any one is weak, the entire mechanism may topple over.

As this book will reveal, journalistic learning is an approach to education that taps into each component, fueling all students' intrinsic motivation. Through project-based journalistic assignments, students engage in the autonomy-supportive activity of selecting topics to research and individuals to interview. Exercising these new skills bolsters their confidence and competence. Finally, they work in teams, developing collaborative skills and the ability to advocate their ideas, compromise, and reach a consensus.

KEY TAKEAWAYS

In this chapter, we explored the myth of the "reluctant learner" and how different labels we as parents or teachers apply to our children can stifle their yearning to learn. Fortunately, we also have the power to disrupt these negative descriptors. And while today's classroom has its roots in the industiral revolution—whose setup places a premium on obedient workers, not life-long learners—there are ways teacher and parents can work within an outdated system to instill in students a passion for learning. Journalistic learning, for instance, taps into students' innate interests and allows them to lead their own projects.

QUESTIONS TO CONSIDER

- What labels or terms have you heard used to describe your child at school? How does that term make you feel? How does it make them feel?
- What motivated you to learn in school? What discouraged your learning?
- What topics spark your child's interest? Does your child have opportunities to explore those topics in school?

REFERENCES

Brenan, M. (2021, November 20). *K–12 parents remain largely satisfied with child's education.* Gallup.com. Retrieved March 25, 2023, from https://news.gallup.com/poll/354083/parents-remain-largely-satisfied-child-education.aspx

Deci, E. L., & Ryan, R. M. (2014). *Intrinsic motivation and self-determination in human behavior.* Springer Science+Business Media.

Dweck, C. S. (2006). *Mindset: The new psychology of success.* Random house.

Masters in Special Education Degree Program Guide. (2021, November 9). *5 historical figures who overcame learning disorders.* Retrieved March 25, 2023, from https://www.masters-in-special-education.com/lists/5-historical-figures-who-overcame-learning-disorders/

Pink, D. H. (2011). *Drive.* Penguin Group US.

Chapter 3

Kids Don't Need Fixing

Sara, a sixth-grader in our pilot program, sat in front of the computer screen with a dazed look. She and her peers were assembled in their middle school's library computer lab and assigned to write articles informed by their recent video conversations with experts on self-selected topics.

A week earlier, Sara stood out as a confident and curious researcher, filled with questions for a professional dancer—a subject close to her heart. However, she was at a loss for words when I asked her to write about her discoveries.

Sara had recorded audio of the interview and taken meticulous notes as part of JLI's training to use effective journalistic practices. But she wasn't sure where or how to begin.

Seeking to make sense of the disconnect and to offer some coaching, I kneeled on the floor next to Sara as she continued to struggle.

"I don't know what to write," she said with a troubled look. "I'm afraid I won't get it right."

Hoping our exchange would trigger a starting point, I asked, "What did your interview subject say that you found most memorable?"

"She loves performing more than anything else," Sara recalled with a smile.

"Write that," I said.

She looked puzzled, as though somehow that would be breaking the rules. While our writing tools have evolved, I quickly realized that much about how we often teach writing has yet to. Unlike working with typewriters, word processing software allows us to write how we think—out of order—as our ideas flow. We can begin an article wherever inspiration strikes and go back later to reorganize our thoughts.

Sara believed she needed to get it right the first time. This misguided quest for immediate perfection stops many beginning writers from thriving. Simply letting go of this limiting belief allowed Sara to experience a new sense of freedom about her assignment.

But why do so many school-aged children develop this need to get it right in the first place? What drives this desire for perfection?

One factor may be America's work culture, which glorifies competition and a fierce dedication to one's job. In 2014, for instance, Gallup found half of full-time U.S. employees worked more than 40 hours a week. Twenty-one percent reported working 50 hours or more (Saad, 2023).

America idolizes overachievers, and clearly, our celebrity culture does too. Entrepreneurs, athletes, and filmmakers, many of whom identify as perfectionists, have emerged as "stars" to emulate. Take the much-revered Steve Jobs. Despite his brilliance, the Apple cofounder infamously tormented his creative team with his endless tweaking. In his biography of the business magnate, Walter Isaacson revealed no detail was too insignificant to escape Jobs's critical gaze, not even the inner workings of Apple computers.

"Look at the memory chips. That's ugly. The lines are too close together," Jobs bemoaned of the initial Macintosh circuit board design, despite the fact those aesthetically displeasing lines would remain unseen by consumers. Jobs even had his own creative team's signatures inscribed inside the legendary computer seeing his products as works of art (Isaacson, 2011).

Perfectionism demands a high level of scrutiny, often directed at one's own work. Tennis superstar Serena Williams can attest to that. She once spoke about her tendency to get frustrated with herself on the court during a 2020 post-match conference. Williams, the winner of 23 Grand Slam singles and one of the world's most celebrated athletes, traced her perfectionist roots to memorizing the alphabet at four.

"I stayed up and kept erasing it until I got it perfect," she told reporters. "I remember I woke up the next day, and I didn't finish my homework because I kept erasing it. That's been the story of my life" (Graham, 2020).

William's drive to play every match to perfection is a crucial reason for her success, but even she admits she can be too hard on herself. She even sees her young daughter mirroring her behavior.

Tennis was one of the few things they could do safely together during the COVID lockdown, but Williams initially thought she'd never let her child play, considering the sport's high demands. She worried about the pressure.

Undoubtedly, America's trumpeted (and occasionally derided) work culture contributes to this heightened pressure, whether it's in sports, business, or the arts. However, as the rest of this chapter will outline, parents are often the primary purveyors of these perfectionist attitudes in their children. This is by no means a critique of families who work incredibly hard, often with limited means, to set their children up for success. It is a natural endeavor worthy of admiration, not criticism.

Instead, this chapter acknowledges how even well-meaning parents can imprint these unhealthy perfectionist habits on their children. Some parents unintentionally value good grades more than qualities that support well-roundedness and life-long learning, like curiosity and independence. Sometimes overemphasis on academic success starts before their child is even born.

THE MOZART EFFECT

The much-touted (and highly dubious) "Mozart effect" is a perfect example of this well-intentioned but misguided pursuit. It all started in 1993 when researchers published a study in *Nature* exploring the relationship between music cognition and spatial reasoning—the ability to visualize objects and recognize their spatial relations accurately.

In the study, college students who listened to 10 minutes of a Mozart piano sonata before a test performed significantly better than their peers who prepared without the classical composer's aid (Rauscher et al., 1993).

The implications were, of course, limited. The test assessed spatial reasoning, not general intelligence, and the purported "Mozart effect" was only temporary, which researchers noted in their study. However, that didn't stop a media frenzy that, like a game of telephone, gradually distorted researchers' findings with each successive headline. The understanding soon became that children could improve their intelligence by simply listening to classical music. Some mothers even believed cranking up Mozart could benefit babies still in the womb.

The belief in Mozart's power to spark intelligence became widespread, shaping fiscal policy. In 1998, Georgia's governor Zell Miller proposed spending $105,000 to send the state's newborns home with classical CD compilations. Miller even played a tape-recorded excerpt of Beethoven's "Ode to Joy" during a January budget address to sway skeptics.

"Now don't you feel smarter already?" Miller asked state lawmakers. "Smart enough to vote for this budget item, I hope," (Sack, 1998).

Reviews of such studies exploring the relationship between music and cognitive performance have similarly found the "Mozart effect" to be temporary while only modestly improving spatial reasoning skills. The phenomenon is also not exclusive to classical music.

The notion that Eurocentric art provides young people more benefits than works from other parts of the world is itself problematic, perpetuating the myth that these classical pieces hold more cultural value than folk or indigenous art. Mozart, the musical genius he was, held no special intelligence-granting powers.

But the myth persisted. In 1996, suburban mother Julie Aigner-Clark started her own baby entertainment production company partially based on this premise. Her *Baby Einstein* video series, with colorful puppets, toys, and classical music, garnered a voracious audience of parents eager to expand their child's intellect (Graham, 2017).

Many parents hoped their babies would discern foreign languages by watching a 30-minute video like *Language Nursery*. Or, similarly, watch a video like *Baby Mozart* and gain an appreciation for the composer's creative genius.

Despite no evidence, infants pick up foreign words from watching a video or, for that matter, acquire a taste for Bach's *Goldberg Variations* from watching *Baby Bach*, Baby Einstein's popularity soared. In a few short years, the once modest production company grew into a multimillion dollar operation, reporting sales as high as $30 million. Aigner-Clark later sold *Baby Einstein* to the Walt Disney Company.

To her credit, Aigner-Clark dismissed the notion that her videos sparked genius. "We don't claim the products will make your children smarter, but they might enrich their lives," she told the *Denver Business Journal* in 2002 (Mook, 2002).

Whether or not parents got the message was a different story. *Baby Einstein* soon expanded into books, toy lines, and even flashcards. At one point, nearly a third of American children (6 years or younger) had seen at least one *Baby Einstein* video, according to a 2003 Kaiser Family Foundation study (Lewin, 2003).

The same study found nearly half of surveyed parents considered these videos "very important" to their child's intellectual development. Even George W. Bush jumped on the *Baby Einstein* train, praising Aiger-Clark's entrepreneurial spirit in his 2007 State of the Union address.

Baby Einstein had undoubtedly swept the nation. However, with rising popularity came questions over the series' efficacy. Were videos like *Language Nursery* and *Baby Mozart* actually improving early childhood development? Studies increasingly disputed that claim.

In 2006, the Campaign for Commercial-Free Childhood, an advocacy group aiming to curb marketers' influence on children, directed the Federal Trade Commission to review Disney's claims of *Baby Einstein*'s educational value. As a result, Disney dropped "educational" from the product's marketing (Graham, 2017).

But the CCFC wasn't finished. In 2009, the advocacy group, aided by the threat of a class-action lawsuit, forced Disney to offer more than $110 million in refunds to parents for false advertising. Disney eventually sold *Baby Einstein* to another toy manufacturer (Lewin, 2009).

While the brand continues to sell items billed as infant developmental products, the myth that one can simply set their child up for success by playing a video or music has hopefully faded. But many parents still hope to find a suitable video series or learn the proper technique to "fix" their child.

Psychologist Frances Rauscher, one of the authors of the original 1993 music study, believed this desire for "quick fixes" to steer children toward success is what fueled the "Mozart effect" craze from the beginning.

"I mean [parents] want to do everything they possibly can for their children," Rauscher told NPR in 2010. She believed if parents thought something as simple as playing Mozart would give their child an advantage in school, they would do it (Spiegel, 2010).

BABY IVIES

Many families look for that advantage in preschool. Take parents in affluent communities across the country. In major cities like Los Angeles and Seattle, parents with the best intentions go to extreme lengths to admit their children into so-called "Baby Ivies," elite preschools boasting top-of-the-line extracurriculars like chess and yoga.

According to one 2018 *Business Insider* story about New York's competitive nursery school market, Baby Ivies are so exclusive some desperate parents pay a "preschool consultant" thousands to help their 3 or 4-year-old gain admission.

Applications for spots can be quite comprehensive, including interviews with parents and an extensive essay (not written by the toddler, of course) detailing their family values and their child's interests. This is quite a feat, considering many 20-year-old college graduates still don't know what they want to do (Gross, 2018). However, open slots for many of the Big Apple's elite nurseries can be hard to come by. Many schools adopt a lottery system, leaving some parents to take more creative approaches to win admission.

In 2002, the New York Attorney General's office investigated a Wall Street telecommunications analyst for his sudden positive reevaluation of AT&T shares. The sudden change allegedly helped a Citigroup executive, who in turn secured his twin children highly coveted spots at New York City's 92nd Street Y Nursery School (Morgenson & McGeehan, 2002).

The nursery certainly is exclusive—and expensive. Currently, tuition for 4 and 5-year-olds attending full-day classes costs parents over $39,000. Just for perspective, the average cost of tuition for a public college in the 2020 academic year, according to a *U.S. News* analysis, was $21,000 (Kerr & Wood, 2022).

Often the real draw for parents is a program's prestige. Parents hope these elite preschools launch their children into elite elementary schools and so on, aiming to get their children admitted into highly selective universities.

HIGH ANXIETY

But what message does this send to children? Certainly not a confidence-building one. Suburban students, usually considered free from the problems and mental health challenges often plaguing their disadvantaged peers, report crushing anxiety and depression just like other students. But why? Many live in wealthy communities, attend generously funded high schools, and don't have to worry about paying for college, let alone paying for their next meal.

Mental health, however, isn't just tied to abundant resources. In fact, in one surprising 1999 study, researcher and clinical psychologist Suniya Luthar found students at a high school in a Connecticut suburb (mostly white and affluent) reported significantly higher anxiety and substance use levels than their peers at an inner-city high school.

While privileged in their upbringing, Luthar discovered these students felt enormous pressure from their parents to achieve academically. They also felt emotionally detached, reporting their parents emphasized doing well in school over their mental well-being (Luthar & D'Avanzo, 1999). The consequences of this constant pressure for perfection included increased anxiety and depression.

For some students, this level of pressure leads to tragedy. In 2016, the city of Palo Alto, home to the rich and highly competitive Silicon Valley community, reported a teen suicide rate four times the national average, with 10 deaths over 7 years. That figure sparked a Centers for Disease Control investigation, but many Santa Clara County students already viewed the pressure for academic excellence as a contributing factor (Lynch, 2016).

It's not uncommon for these students to take on an exhausting course load of rigorous Advanced Placement courses to please their parents. One or two in a given semester is sensible, but a schedule that includes several demanding science courses can quickly overwhelm young people. However, journalistic courses often provide them with a creative outlet for self-expression.

During my observation visits to Palo Alto High School, I met several students who told me after-school news production sessions became a safe haven from the pressures of their parents' scrutiny. They could be themselves and pursue any story that captured their imaginations.

They weren't "competing" for high marks but exploring wherever their inspirations took them.

It's important to remember the pressure to succeed academically can be compounded for marginalized students. Many who took their lives in Santa Clara County were Asian American. Helen Hsu, a psychologist at Stanford and former president of the Asian American Psychologists Association, argued cultural and identity issues facing Asian American students added to their mental health struggles (Lynch, 2016).

It's not uncommon for immigrants and marginalized people to become demanding parents. One 2012 Johns Hopkins University study found children of immigrants significantly outperformed peers whose parents were born in the United States. The study's authors pointed to, among other reasons, the higher expectations immigrant parents placed on their children to succeed (Lunday, 2012).

Faced with these facts, many parents ask themselves some form of this question: "Why am I driven, sometimes to the point of obsession, to ensure my child succeeds?" A deeper question might be: "Are my best intentions possibly harming my child?" Self-exploration around the first question often leads parents to reflect on how their own parents engaged with them about grades and test scores. Chances are, if your parents were taskmasters, you might be inclined to replicate that behavior with your offspring. If that's the case, think back on what it was like when your report card arrived home. If the memory is unpleasant, ask yourself if you truly want to induce that same anxiety in your own child.

Conversely, you may remember your parents as being too lenient. Left to your own devices, perhaps you didn't consider yourself a "good student" and therefore feel that you missed opportunities and underachieved. Psychology suggests that we grow to emulate or rebel against our parents' behavioral patterns. It's that desire to "be just like them, or never ever be like them," depending on our assessment of how well their parenting practices affected our lives.

It's fair to say neither you nor your parents are completely at fault for behaviors that don't support children's well-being. Cultural factors play a role. First, product marketing conditions us to measure our "success" compared to others. Long before television ads that taught consumers to measure their self-worth by the size of their homes or the cars they drove, a 1912 comic strip called "Keeping up with the Joneses" popularized social climbing and a need to "keep up" with one's neighbors.

By the time television advertisers realized the power of this strategy, the importance of "keeping score" had permeated American culture. Older generations remember a time when paying for clothing that featured corporate branding was unthinkable. Today, our willingness to be a human billboard costs a premium and is considered a sign of prestige.

Our children get the memo at a very early age. They "must have" sneakers that cost $150 rather than an unpopular functional brand that just might be better made. So many parents are willing to go into debt to "keep up" and unwittingly model behaviors their children are likely to repeat as adults.

This conversation is not meant to be a downer or inflict parental guilt. Societal pressures are powerful and pervasive. It takes courage to break the cycle and to teach our children their self-worth need not be tied to the price of their shoes or sweatshirt. A child who feels *whole* doesn't seek external validation or the need to impress peers. They also emerge as resilient in the face of the inevitable uncertainty of life, better prepared to navigate change. Material possessions aren't the only source of societal pressures that adversely affect our kids. The ability to share heavily filtered snapshots from our everyday lives online is undoubtedly another factor.

SOCIAL MEDIA'S IMPACT

Whether scrolling through photos of a friend's vacation to Rome on Instagram or reading about another friend's admission to Harvard in a Facebook update, social media always reminds us of why we aren't perfect *enough*.

In an interview, one of my university students, Mackenzie, recalled that Instagram was becoming "a thing" when she was entering middle school. By age 14, she grieved regularly, troubled by insecurities about her body image.

"I was always a bit taller and stockier than my friends," she said. "I was wearing 'large' sized clothing while everyone else was wearing 'small' or 'extra small.'" Subtle unintended messages from her friend group exacerbated Mackenzie's anxiety about her looks.

"I remember, as we hit fifth or sixth grade, my friends and I would meet up in matching outfits to take pictures," she said. "I became obsessed about how I looked. However, when we went out it was usually, 'hey Mackenzie, will you take the picture?'" She soon realized she rarely appeared in the photos friends were posting. Mackenzie was hospitalized briefly when she entered high school to address severe anxiety and depression. She deleted her social media accounts and developed a healthier sense of self, no longer tied to peer comparisons.

We now know that Mackenzie's story is fairly common. In 2021, Facebook whistleblower France Haugen testified before Congress about internal memos that appear to confirm parents' worse fears about the adverse effects of some social media content on teen mental health. Young girls are particularly prone to experience ill effects. Leaked internal Facebook documents indicate that 13.5% of U.K. teen girls said Instagram worsened their suicidal thoughts. Another leaked study found 17% of teen girls said their eating disorders worsened after Instagram use (Romo, 2021).

Nichole Kelly is an associate professor who researches how pervasive societal messages about weight and body image can adversely affect teens, particularly girls. "The media broadly, and more so now social media, plays a really big role in defining appearance ideals. They've been a player for a long time in perpetuating expectations and ideals about the way a person 'should' look," Kelly said. She recommends encouraging young people to pay more attention to how they feel after engaging with social media. "If it leaves you feeling bad about yourself, notice that, and consider disengaging, even if for only a few days," Kelly said.

This is not to minimize the potential benefits of social media. In fact, in 2018 Pew Research found 68% of teens said these platforms made them feel connected to others who could support them during tough times. However, that same survey found 43% of teens felt pressure to only post content casting them in a positive light. Thirty-seven percent wanted only to post content garnering likes and comments (Anderson & Jiang, 2018).

In other words, in the social media world, teenagers feel the heat to impress their peers and their parents. This explains why studies have linked social media use among adolescents to low self-esteem and depression. So much so, in 2022 the Seattle Public School district took the unprecedented step of suing TiTok, Instagram, Snapchat, Facebook, and Youtube for the alleged ill effects of their algorithms on teen mental health. The complaint stated, "Defendants have successfully exploited the vulnerable brains of youth, hooking tens of millions of students across the country into positive feedback loops of excessive use and abuse of Defendants' social media platforms" (Reuters, 2023).

Countering the potential adverse effects of social media on adolescents is no easy feat. Algorithms learn to anticipate our wants and needs and offer easy and immediate antidotes. Also, teens are savvy at evading nearly all attempts to monitor their activity by covering their tracks. Desirous of maintaining their privacy, young people set up dummies and multiple accounts.

The illusion that what you post will "disappear" leads to teen sexting and behaviors that can damage a child for life.

So, what is a concerned parent to do? The specifics are worthy of a whole separate book. However, there are some basics to distill here.

First, it is crucial to understand the "need" that social media fills for teens and adults. At the heart of the matter, social media "likes" can provide us with an illusive sense of *belonging*, which social psychologists have determined is a basic human need.

When this need is unfulfilled, we will likely seek it externally and in artificial ways. True *friendships* can become complicated. Misunderstandings can lead to temporary and sometimes irreconcilable conflicts resulting in painful breakups. It's much easier to click or unclick "like" than to confront differences, own our role in transgressions, and reach resolutions. Yet, instinctively, this is how we truly grow as individuals, whether separately or together. "Digital break-ups," whether romantic or with a close friend, rarely soothe or satisfy our hearts.

Science now confirms that emotional pain and physical pain share the same neural pathways, activating similar areas of our brains. In one study, 40 individuals experiencing recent breakups were shown images of their ex-partners. As they reflected on their relationships, areas of their brains associated with physical pain lit up during medical scans. Conversely, Tylenol (the over-the-counter pain reliever) has been shown to reduce emotional hurt (Young, 2020).

Addressing emotional conflicts, face-to-face can be highly stressful, if not threatening. Our desire to follow a path of least resistance wishes for anything but confronting such situations head-on. Yet emotional pain is an unavoidable fact of being alive. How else can we learn from our misjudgments of others' character, better identify our blind spots, and understand our sense of self?

Instead, social media posts would lead the world to believe our lives are perfect—a collection of idyllic backdrops, people, and poses. We're programmed to project a myth rather than accept reality. A generation that fails to accept that life can and will get messy is potentially destined for greater disappointments.

Whether we've lost the ability to find satisfaction in candid images of ourselves is a wonder. Will this generation miss out on the experience of rummaging through old "goofball" photos of oneself? Photos where you allowed yourself to be yourself—imperfections and all. Or will all self-portraits be reduced to hyper-posed moments? Glancing forward, pursed lips, stomachs in? All boringly predictable poses? All the same?

One must also wonder whether we'll even be able to locate photo memories of our past. As photo albums gave way to Facebook sharing, we no longer collect or possess personal memorabilia and haven't for some time. What happens if Facebook eventually goes the way of Friendster? Or if you tire of the platform or disagree with its corporate agenda and opt to delete your account? Individuals over 30 relate to having a drawer full of old drives incompatible with current technology. From time to time, many of us come across a discarded drive in a drawer with obsolete cable connectors. What irretrievable long-forgotten memories might they hold? Who knows?

For many, strikingly sharp digital images are just too real—revealing blemishes and imperfections we would rather conceal. Enter filters, Photoshop, and image manipulation software designed to "enhance" your appeal. As teens discover Tinder and other relationship apps, the desire to craft a perfect profile can intensify. A little embellishment or a small fabrication can lead to an unintended outcome. Over time, there's a disconnect between your "ideal" narrative and who shows up for that first date. The risk is becoming a foolhearty person who's out of touch with reality.

People magazine is littered with stories of celebrities who spend thousands of dollars attempting to halt aging's natural effects. Commercials tell us to shade our gray, tuck our tummies, and present unsustainable images of our carefully crafted "best selves." It's a trap that leads to an inevitable question. Do we want to raise kids who are comfortable in their own skin or strive to achieve some unrealistic state of perfection?

THE PERFECTIONIST TRAP

Understandably, parents want the best for their children, and it's important to recognize perfectionism isn't necessarily a bad trait. Encouraging students to earn good grades and set high goals can be positive. What's more, the desire to refine one's skills and make the best possible version of a creative project—a painting, a company logo, or even a news article—is a terrific motivating force.

But if perfectionism can be a driver for learning, at what point does it become harmful? The research tells us this is when we become more concerned with avoiding failure than achieving success.

Striving for academic perfection indeed benefits some students, but unfortunately, some take it too far. A student obsessed with getting the perfect grade frets failing his biology test more than understanding how photosynthesis actually works. A student too afraid of making writing mistakes on her *Grapes of Wrath* term paper refuses to share her draft with a peer to get helpful edits.

In short, unhealthy perfectionism harms learning by encouraging fixed mindsets in students. Instead of seeing errors on a paper as an opportunity to further improve their writing, a student preoccupied with achieving perfection sees these errors as indicators of insurmountable deficits. When students begin to tie their identity to their grades, a series of bad marks can fuel their anxiety. They didn't make mistakes; they *are* the mistake.

Unfortunately, more and more young people are falling into this perfectionist trap.

Jessica Naeker, a clinical psychologist at the Aspiring Families Center for Mental Health and Wellness in San Diego, argues that when young people feel significant pressure to live up to these high expectations, especially early in their development, they can develop serious mental issues and health problems (Maker, 2018).

It's no wonder 70% of American teenagers told the Pew Research Center in 2018 that anxiety and depression were significant issues facing their peers. The results held across gender, racial and socioeconomic boundaries (Horowitz & Graf, 2020).

The same Pew survey found 61% of teens felt pressure to succeed *academically*, while only 29% felt pressure to *look good*, and 28% felt pressure to fit in socially (Horowitz & Graf, 2020). The stereotypical view of carefree teenagers concerned more with popularity than earning straight A's never looked so outdated.

OUR TESTING OBSESSION

It's also worth exploring how the culture of over-testing, which has dominated education policy in the past two decades, has further imperiled students' confidence. Take No Child Left Behind. Signed into law in 2002, this education package required states to test students in math and reading from third to eighth grade and once in high school. Schools failing to stay on track toward meeting their prescribed proficiency goals on said tests faced the consequences, like stronger state intervention or shutdowns.

Further, policies like Race to the Top expanded testing, compelling states to adopt stricter standards for academic performance and spurring the creation of the Common Core State Standards initiative. The initiative aimed to bring students on the same page nationwide in math and language arts benchmarks. Standardized assessments were now used as early as kindergarten.

This expansion sparked a backlash from educators. In 2015, the Alliance for Childhood, which promotes improved early childhood education, released a report criticizing the Common Core's early reading standards for kindergartners and the initiative more broadly. The report asserted children in kindergarten are not developmentally ready to fully acquire reading skills (Carlsson-Paige et al., 2015).

Furthermore, researchers highlighted the benefits of play-based kindergarten classrooms where children can explore their interests and socialize with peers. Academic-centered programs, while boosting young kindergarteners' test scores in the short term, proved to be harmful to their overall development in the long run.

At the far end of the K–12 spectrum, standardized tests add yet another high-stakes hurdle for high schoolers to jump through. Many students already stress over earning the perfect SAT and ACT scores, hoping to land in the percentile of test-takers most favorable to their dream school. The amount of sweat, tears, and sleepless nights students put into a three-hour test, which many hinge their college hopes on, can be overwhelming. Many parents, highly invested in their child's success on that one test, hire SAT tutors to help their students prepare. Then, there are headline-making incidents where parents with means have "fixed" the scores afterward.

Actress Felicity Huffman pleaded guilty to such a crime in 2019 following a widely reported college admissions scandal that ensnared dozens of high-profile parents who paid millions in bribes to land their children at elite schools. Huffman herself paid an SAT proctor $15,000 to change her daughter's score following the test.

"My daughter knew absolutely nothing about my actions, and in my misguided and profoundly wrong way, I have betrayed her," Huffman admitted in her first public statement on the matter nearly a month after the admissions scandal broke (Atkinson, 2019).

How does this level of testing help our children succeed? Are we not just telling them they can only derive self-worth from earning a perfect SAT score?

When toddlers are scrutinized as early as four, their confidence can suffer. That's when children focus more on end results, like learning how to ace a multiple-choice math test, rather than appreciating the learning journey itself. Often, this journey is not always a straight line. One standardized test in kindergarten won't predict where your child will be in sixth grade.

NO "FIXING" REQUIRED

All parents and teachers want to see their children lead successful and productive lives (it's probably why you're reading this book). However, the fear that one's child may fall behind, whether in a particular class or among their peers, has driven many desperate parents to overcompensate based on false concerns.

A few years ago, I attended one of the book promotions of my colleague Esther Wojcicki's bestseller, *How to Raise Successful Children*. As I mentioned earlier, Esther is a Journalistic Learning Initiative cofounder who led Palo Alto High School's renowned journalism program for 37 years.

Following her presentation, during the Q&A session, one mother asked how her daughter could improve her focus in grade school. Esther, after all, is the mother of three successful daughters: Susan, the former CEO of YouTube; Anne, the founder and CEO of the genetic testing company 23 and Me; and Janet, a distinguished anthropologist, and epidemiologist.

Surely, Esther placed high expectations on her children and intimately involved herself in their education. How did she push them to succeed in school? How did she motivate them?

"How old is your daughter?" Esther asked the mother.

"Eleven," she responded. The audience giggled.

"I think you should cut her some slack. Trust me, she won't ruin her life if she's not completely focused at age eleven."

Amid the turmoil of keeping our children safe, well fed, and getting them to school on time, we often forget the importance of giving them opportunities to derive knowledge for themselves.

In her book, Esther described giving her grade-school-aged grandchildren such an opportunity while shopping for school supplies. She simply dropped them off at Target and allowed them to find their paper, pencils, and binders independently. They could call her when they finished.

"They're more of an expert than I am," Esther said. "They've been to Target with me a lot." Esther's daughter later called to inquire about her children's whereabouts. She was momentarily shocked by her mother's decision, but her children indeed called back when they were finished, just as Esther predicted (Wojcicki, 2019).

Children need room to make their own decisions and learn from their mistakes. That's what's so essential about early learning programs like preschool and kindergarten. These spaces allow children to play and explore. They nurture their curiosity.

The Journalistic Learning Initiative doesn't demand students be perfect or that students like Sarah, the sixth-grader I saw struggling in front of her computer, write her story according to a prescribed formula. Our programs allow students to explore, make mistakes, and work collaboratively on long-term projects.

Crucially, these projects allow students to consistently redraft their work, freeing them from the pressure to get everything right on the first try. They encourage students to share their work with peers and receive constructive feedback. And it is their work. Students pursue their interests just like Sarah did when interviewing a professional dancer.

Journalism is all about curiosity. It acknowledges the limitlessness of our understanding. There's always something new to learn, a new angle to a story, and a new approach to solving a problem. Journalistic learning doesn't assume a student's knowledge is fixed. It is based on a presumption that children "don't need fixing," and that to spark their motivation, we must put students in the driver's seat of their learning. It's okay if they make a few detours along the way.

KEY TAKEAWAYS

This chapter explored the various forces pressuring students to be perfect—to "get it right on the first try." From living in a country obsessed with long work hours and standardized testing, to consuming a strict media diet of Instagram posts and Facebook updates, more and more young people are falling into perfectionist traps. Unfortunately, well-meaning parents can push their children into these traps too. Whether its preoccupation with good grades or getting their child into the best college (or even the best preschool), parents can unintentionally fuel their child's anxiety. Students need to be challenged, of course. But students aren't really focused on learning if they're more worried about making a mistake. Children need to learn that mistakes are okay. We as parents and teachers need to create environments for children where they feel safe to be creative and take risks.

QUESTIONS TO CONSIDER

- What forces do you see putting pressure on your child? *School work? Career planning? Social media use?*
- How does your child react to bad grades? Do they feel discouraged? Motivated to do better?

- Does your child find it difficult to start certain assignments? Why do they find it challenging?

REFERENCES

Anderson, M., & Jiang, J. (2018, November 28). *Teens' social media habits and experiences*. Pew Research Center: Internet, Science & Tech. Retrieved March 25, 2023, from https://www.pewresearch.org/internet/2018/11/28/teens-social-media-habits-and-experiences/

Atkinson, K. (2019, April 8). *Actress Felicity Huffman among 13 parents to plead guilty in admissions scandal*. Axios. Retrieved March 25, 2023, from https://www.axios.com/2019/04/08/felicity-huffman-college-admissions-scandal

Carlsson-Paige, N., McLaughlin, G., & Almon, J. (2015). *Reading Instruction in Kindergarten: Little to Gain and Much to Lose*. https://www.google.com/url?sa=t&rct=j&q=&esrc=s&source=web&cd=&ved=2ahUKEwi-i9mS6YH-AhV8BzQIHd-KCiEQFnoECBEQAQ&url=https%3A%2F%2Ffiles.eric.ed.gov%2Ffulltext%2FED609172.pdf&usg=AOvVaw1DYa8723mUEICOTnsgwjB7

Graham, M. (2020, September 4). *"I'm a perfectionist—it's the story of my life," admits Serena Williams*. Tennishead. Retrieved March 25, 2023, from https://tennishead.net/im-a-perfectionist-it-has-been-the-story-of-my-life-admits-serena-williams-after-us-open-win/

Graham, R. (2017, December 19). *Once upon a time, parents thought videos of puppets playing Mozart would make babies smarter*. Slate Magazine. Retrieved March 25, 2023, from https://slate.com/technology/2017/12/the-rise-and-fall-of-baby-einstein.html

Gross, E. L. (2018). *Inside the insanely competitive world of elite New York City preschools*. Business Insider. Retrieved March 25, 2023, from https://www.businessinsider.com/preschools-in-new-york-city-2018-6

Horowitz, J. M., & Graf, N. (2020, May 30). *Most U.S. teens see anxiety and depression as a major problem among their peers*. Pew Research Center's Social & Demographic Trends Project. Retrieved March 25, 2023, from https://www.pewresearch.org/social-trends/2019/02/20/most-u-s-teens-see-anxiety-and-depression-as-a-major-problem-among-their-peers/

Isaacson, W. (2011). *Steve Jobs*. Simon & Schuster U.S.

Kerr, E., & Wood, S. (2022, September 12). *See the average college tuition in 2021–2022—US News & World Report*. (n.d.). Retrieved March 25, 2023, from https://www.usnews.com/education/best-colleges/paying-for-college/articles/paying-for-college-infographic

Lewin, T. (2003, October 29). *A growing number of video viewers watch from Crib*. The New York Times. Retrieved March 25, 2023, from https://www.nytimes.com/2003/10/29/us/a-growing-number-of-video-viewers-watch-from-crib.html

Lewin, T. (2009, October 24). *No Einstein in your crib? Get a refund.* The New York Times. Retrieved March 25, 2023, from https://www.nytimes.com/2009/10/24/education/24baby.html

Lunday, A. (2012, September 13). *Children of U.S. immigrants outperforming their peers, study shows.* The Hub. Retrieved March 25, 2023, from https://hub.jhu.edu/2012/09/13/immigrant-children-study/

Luthar S. S., D'Avanzo K. (1999). Contextual factors in substance use: A study of suburban and inner-city adolescents. *Development and Psychopathology.* 11:845–867.

Lynch, G. H. (2016, May 2). *The CDC is investigating a cluster of teen suicides in Palo Alto.* The World from PRX. Retrieved March 25, 2023, from https://theworld.org/stories/2016-05-02/cdc-investigating-cluster-teen-suicides-palo-alto

Maker, A. H. (2018, September 30). *The perils of perfectionism in kids and teens.* Psychology Today. Retrieved March 25, 2023, from https://www.psychologytoday.com/us/blog/helping-kids-cope/201809/the-perils-of-perfectionism-in-kids-and-teens

Mook, B. (2002). *In a 'tot'-anic size '01 deal, Disney buys Baby Einstein.* Bizjournals.com. (n.d.). Retrieved March 27, 2023, from https://www.bizjournals.com/denver/stories/2002/03/04/focus9.html

Morgenson, G., & Mcgeehan, P. (2002, November 14). *Wall st. and the Nursery School: A New York Story.* The New York Times. Retrieved March 25, 2023, from https://www.nytimes.com/2002/11/14/business/wall-st-and-the-nursery-school-a-new-york-story.html

Rauscher, F., Shaw, G., & Ky, C. (1993). Music and spatial task performance. *Nature* 365, 611. https://doi.org/10.1038/365611a0

Reuters. (2023, January 9). *Seattle Public Schools Blame Tech Giants for social media harm in lawsuit.* Reuters. Retrieved March 25, 2023, from https://www.reuters.com/technology/seattle-public-schools-blame-tech-giants-social-media-harm-lawsuit-2023-01-08/

Romo, V. (2021, October 5). *Whistleblower's testimony has resurfaced Facebook's Instagram problem.* NPR. Retrieved March 25, 2023, from https://www.npr.org/2021/10/05/1043194385/whistleblowers-testimony-facebook-instagram

Saad, L. (2023, January 23). *The "40-hour" workweek is actually longer—by seven hours.* Gallup.com. Retrieved March 25, 2023, from https://news.gallup.com/poll/175286/hour-workweek-actually-longer-seven-hours.aspx

Sack, K. (1998, January 15). *Georgia's governor seeks musical start for babies*. *The New York Times*. Retrieved March 25, 2023, from https://www.nytimes.com/1998/01/15/us/georgia-s-governor-seeks-musical-start-for-babies.html

Spiegel, A. (2010, June 28). *"Mozart effect" was just what we wanted to hear*. NPR. Retrieved March 25, 2023, from https://www.npr.org/2010/06/28/128104580/mozart-effect-was-just-what-we-wanted-to-hear

Wojcicki, E. (2019). *How to raise successful people: Simple lessons for radical results*. Hutchinson.

Young, K. (2020, August 6). *Your body during a breakup: The science of a broken heart*. Hey Sigmund. Retrieved March 25, 2023, from https://www.heysigmund.com/your-body-during-a-breakup/

Chapter 4

Flipping the Switch

In this chapter, I explore how parents and teachers can inspire students to transition from passive learners to self-determined acquirers of new knowledge. Rather than being "schooled," they emerge as active co-designers of their education. A shift in consciousness occurs, where students begin to realize their capacity to assume ownership of their futures. You'll meet students and teachers engaged in collaborative processes where power is shared rather than enforced.

As I shared in this book's introduction, having a mom who also taught grade school afforded me many benefits. She knew how the educational "system" worked and how to make the most of it. She also modeled assertiveness strategies I learned and continue to emulate. "Don't be timid. Look them in the eye, and ask for what you want," she would say.

Black families with Southern roots like ours learned these lessons the hard way and with an extra sense of precaution. A misstep could be catastrophic, costing your job and community reputation. You develop instincts about timing and approach. When is it best to assert yourself and in which ways? The same was true for many ethnically-diverse families viewed as "others" by America's dominant culture.

An example is Sylvia. Nearing age 40, she recalls being raised by a father who worked as a mechanic and truck driver. Refusing to be limited by just an eighth-grade education, he made sacrifices to give Sylvia, her siblings, and her mom a better life.

"Mechanically, he was a whiz and could take anything apart and put it back together, and was really useful for that reason on the sharecropping land that they had. He was able to exert his self-worth in his own ways," she said.

Syliva's was among six million Black families, including mine that participated in the "great migration" North, seeking to escape Southern prejudice and Jim Crow laws.

"They were determined to move and to live different lives, and I'm grateful," she shared. "I think if I had been raised in the South I would have had a different mindset. That's not to say there aren't people who push against the system in the South. But there is something about being raisd in Brooklyn, New York, because it's 'in the air;' this desire to fight to push to battle to continue to kick doors in to make change was in the atmosphere."

After shared military service careers, Sylvia and her husband divorced and she was suddenly a single parent. Sylvia and the kids settled in an affluent suburban Maryland community. The setting was near idyllic, except her two sons and daughter soon discovered they were among the few Black students at their new schools.

Within months, Sylvia began to suspect that her children were being held to a different standard than their peers. "In elementary school, at the lunch table, just fooling around, my oldest son and his friends would sometimes swing their legs and kick each other," she shared. "I remember getting a call at work, saying he was in the principal's office for kicking at lunch."

After confirming that her son and the others were alright, she began asking questions. "I guess they just thought I was going to say 'okay.' Why would I do that?" She pressed the matter further.

She learned that of the several kids involved, only her son was detained in the principal's office for the rest of the day. The decision amounted to in-school suspension, depriving her son of class instruction.

"Why? I went from zero to one hundred, real quick," she recalls.

"The conversation went from me speaking with an administrator in the elementary school office to the vice principal to the principal, and then me leaving to go to the school shortly after those conversations and have a face-to-face conversation," she recalled. "This is my mother in me, and it's also me, building on that foundation of 'Thou shalt not, not with my child.'"

"It was imbalanced because he was the only student in the principal's office," she said. "Now, again, I wasn't there. I don't know what happened. But I know you can't get into a kicking fight under the lunchroom table by yourself."

Sylvia elaborated further about why the administrator's account didn't add up. "The fact that there wasn't anybody else being held in the same regard as him was an immediate flag for me. And when we were done, he went back to class."

Of course, not all transgressions are attributable to overt racism. The term *implicit bias* refers to the unintentional blindspots many people carry regarding matters of equity and inclusion. Well-meaning teachers and administrators from any background can subconsciously act in ways that surprise themselves.

Dayna, a mother who is white, tells a similar parenting story but from the perspective of also working as an educator. After she and her African husband divorced, Dayna was left to single-parent their four biracial children. Keeping two boys and two girls on track to excel while working and attending graduate school was understandably exhausting.

"Both boys seemed to get in more trouble than their friends," she remembers. "I'd get calls; you need to come to school and pick up Terrence or Tyree because one of them had pushed someone in the cafeteria line."

One particular incident stands out. "One of the boys came in from recess with muddy shoes and was labeled 'defiant.' That was the word [administrators] often used."

Graduate school and teaching experience armed Dayna with fact-based ways to respond in these ever-increasing instances.

"I think principals didn't like me because I would turn it back on them with hard data." She cited academic literature that unequivocally indicates the adverse effects of suspending students.

Reflecting on the experiences, Dayna hopes other educators are beginning to understand their role in perpetrating unjust punishment and policies. "They should be asking, 'why is this kid getting five times the referrals as other kids? Why is it the brown kids?'"

Stern phone calls and face-to-face encounters with teachers and administrators aren't for the faint of heart. You may not have had a role model with the moxie to so boldly "speak truth to power," but don't let that stop you from advocating for your child and teaching them to advocate for themselves.

Written communication may be your preferred method. Benefits include sufficient time to collect your thoughts and choose your words carefully. You can also ask another parent or family member to proofread the earliest drafts for tone, composure, and accuracy. Written communication also begins a paper trail, which can be advantageous should your concerns multiply.

You'll want to stick to the facts and maintain a controlled and professional tone, lest you be labeled "hysterical." If the complaint you are communicating is lengthy, don't be limited by email. We're conditioned to skim lengthy emails, causing us to miss finer points. Consider emailing a short introduction, attaching the longer text as a Word document, and mailing a physical copy.

When a parent takes the time to draft and send a well-articulated complaint, it gets teachers' and administrators' attention. In this day and age, mailed written communications are uncommon and demonstrate conviction. Additionally, written communication begins a file on the incident in question, and public employees take files very seriously.

Of course, all communication with schools, whether in-person or written, need not be confrontational.

RETHINKING "COMMUNITY" SCHOOLS

We refer to structures for learning within our neighborhoods as "community schools." However, beyond their locations, very little about how schools are managed feels communal—or democratic. Power dynamics between students and teachers or parents and teachers are rarely equal in public education. The rules of engagement are established from day one. Teachers are beholden to administrative policies that they rarely are invited to codesign, and parents are beholden to report cards that purport to assess their child's knowledge.

While residence within a given school district affords your child admittance, paperwork and procedures tend to reduce students to names and numbers on an attendance roster. Taxed with managing larger classes with fewer resources, many new teachers try but struggle to personalize learning.

We need to rethink the parent-teacher-student relationship to make learning more personalized and responsive to our children's needs. And like all relationships, the most common source of strife is a communication breakdown. So, how can parents and teachers communicate better?

One of the few touch points between you and your child's teacher—if there's an opportunity to touch base—is the iconic and often fretted-over parent-teacher conference. These anticipated (or dreaded) one-on-ones, hosted in a school's library or cafeteria with parents shuffling from one teacher to the next—child occasionally in tow—usually take on a warped significance, and with good reason.

Conferences represent the best chance to learn about your child's presumed skills, behavior, and progress in the classroom. This isn't asking your child at the dinner table how well they did on their science project or what they learned in first-period history (essential dinner conversation, to be sure). This is asking your child's *teacher* questions and hearing objective—and hopefully constructive—insights from the person who works most closely with your child daily.

It's no wonder such meetings gin up anxiety. Conferences seemingly carry lots of weight. At the same time, however, most conferences unfold in a manner that fails to alleviate anxiety or build a relationship between your and your child's teacher, let alone offer an effective way to monitor their progress.

CONFERENCE BREAKDOWN

So what are some of the issues with the current model? To start, teacher/parent conferences are the mechanism school systems have designed to address academic concerns. Most follow a structure we recall from our own school-age experiences and go something like this: a parent sits across from their child's teacher, the teacher gives the parent a summary of the child's performance—how they're doing in class and where their grades stand—and maybe offer suggestions for how their child can make up certain assignments, or continue their progress.

On the surface, this format seems perfectly fine. Parents want to hear directly from their child's educator about their successes and challenges in the classroom. Teachers want to hear directly from parents about their concerns for their students.

But here's the rub: How much can really be accomplished in one 5 to 15-minute sit-down? Parents have limited time to absorb all the important details teachers give about their child's learning goals. What's more, they're hearing from *all* of their child's teachers. That's a lot of information to digest in brief conferences.

Overloaded and overwhelmed, parents can struggle to sift through all the advice. Unfortunately, conferences—as mentioned above—often represent the best chance for teachers and parents to communicate meaningfully. Often, there are few follow-up appointments or opportunities for developing parent-teacher relationships.

Nor is there a chance to include the student in the discussion. If and when a child is present, their role is diminished to simply listening to adults discuss their strengths and presumed "deficiencies." Far from empowering, it objectifies young people, reducing them to the sum total of their "problems."

REIMAGINING THE "CONFERENCE"

It doesn't have to be this way. Conferences, or any kind of meeting with your child's teacher, don't have to be an overload of information in the middle of a frantic shuffle. Parents and teachers can reimagine the conference as the beginning of a meaningful partnership built on clear communication and trust.

In fact, plenty of schools have already worked to reinvent the current conference model. In 2015, for example, researcher Maria C. Paredes of the education nonprofit WestEd helped pilot the parent-teacher team program in a Georgia school district.

At the start of the school year, a teacher met with their class's parents all at once, not separately. During a 90-minute meeting, the teacher laid out key concepts students were expected to learn by the end of the year. Parents then set specific goals for their child on those highlighted skills. Notably, the teacher offered activities parents could practice with their children at home to boost their abilities and set up follow-up one-on-one meetings to evaluate student progress. Piloted in multiple Georgia schools, the program led to greater engagement from parents in their child's academic growth (Sparks, 2020).

Of course, not all schools will have the luxury of time, resources—or a willing administrator—to allow a WestEd researcher to test an innovative program like this in their classrooms. But as a parent, you don't have to wait for outside intervention or even a fall conference to begin creating a productive and meaningful relationship with your child's teacher.

The first meeting with your child's teacher at a conference, at an assembly, or even outside of school can be the foundation for a productive relationship that helps nurture your student's desire to learn.

Before that meeting, set yourself up for success by doing your own homework and researching your teacher's background. This doesn't mean running a background check on your child's public school teacher. (Ideally, the school district has already done this.)

Instead, this first "do-your-homework" step is about showing you're an engaged parent and that you understand what your child's teacher is trying to accomplish in their classroom. This could involve reading course syllabi the teacher has provided your child. It could also include clicking on a teacher's website and reading their bio, assignment deadlines, and the teacher's outlined key learning benchmarks.

Before the meeting, collect your thoughts by listing topics you wish to discuss, such as your child's academic progress, behavior in the classroom, and any special needs or accommodations. Make a note of any issues or concerns you're observing at home. This allows parents and teachers to compare notes.

It's essential to approach the meeting with an open mind and a willingness to listen. Ask the teacher for their perspective and expertise, and avoid jumping to conclusions or making assumptions. Express appreciation for the fact that teaching is challenging work. Your child is one of dozens and, in higher grades, possibly hundreds of other students. Typically, teachers are underresourced and underpaid. So, acknowledging their reality can go a long way.

Instead of attending a conference with little-to-no prep or understanding of an educator's goals, you can be engaged and ready to ask specific questions. Statements like, "In the syllabus, I notice that you emphasize project-based learning . . . " can go a long way in building trust and understanding with the person across the table.

Much too often, conversations between a teacher and parent are complaint-initiated. That is a parent, having just learned of a bad grade, for instance, reaches out to their child's teacher for the first time with the intention of addressing the problem—sometimes with the implication that the teacher was somehow in error or has let their student down.

Breaking the ice with a complaint or accusation doesn't bode well for a fruitful relationship. It creates the expectation for an adversarial one.

Of course, teachers make mistakes, and there are instances where an educator isn't doing enough to respond to a student's needs. Bad apples exist in all professions, and teaching is no exception. However, upon first learning of a problem in the classroom, it's always important to give a teacher some benefit of the doubt, especially when developing a partnership based on trust and clear communication.

STUDENT AGENCY AND TEACHER CONFERENCES

Now that we've put the parent and teacher on equal footing, what about the student? Parent-teacher conferences still typically occur without the child present. Conventional wisdom suggests this is a time for parents to interact directly with teachers that will not shame or embarrass their children. For an excluded student left at home, there can be an anxiety-provoking feeling that your teacher's reports may be a less-than-accurate representation of your concerns or specific needs.

Amazingly, a child may be the last person consulted about why they believe they are struggling to grasp certain concepts or retain fundamental principles. The thought that you're being discussed without your input can be anxiety provoking, even for adults.

In instances when students are invited to attend, there can often be an implicit understanding that they are not welcome to participate. Imagine if two of your supervisors at work invited you to attend your performance review but have yet to address you directly or ask you to speak. It is as though the child is an inanimate piece of furniture in the room. The message, unintentionally, is we don't value your opinion about your education.

It is one of the reasons students can begin to lose interest in school. They can start to believe that teachers and parents don't respect their experiences and concerns. So, what's the point?

A central theme of this book is supporting youth in cultivating their sense of agency. Education experiences shouldn't feel imposed. Rather than being "schooled," students should feel free and empowered to pursue their interests. And habits formed in grade school shape who we become. When we don't instill these values in children, they grow to be individuals who "check the boxes" rather than intentionally pursue their futures.

As college costs continue to rise, students are obligated to play a greater role in designing their academic experiences. Students with sufficient self-awareness and agency will likely have a fulfilling and inspired one. Sadly, most complete the degree requirements but fail to venture beyond prescribed guidelines.

A self-directed learner entering college will make informed choices to maximize the benefits of their investment. They will seek recommendations about professors, request syllabi in advance, attend office hours, and explore extracurricular opportunities. Such students experience college as an ever-fulfilling adventure that stimulates their curiosities and shapes who they become.

Without agency and self-direction, students may never discover professors or classes that would broaden their perspectives. If Apple cofounder Steve Jobs never famously stumbled into a calligraphy class at Reed College, the MacIntosh computer would have looked quite different. Previously, personal computers limited users to working solely with drab green Courier text against a black background. Instead, the MacIntosh featured an array of fonts and graphic capabilities that democratized publishing. So if we want self-directed students, we need to promote agency.

STUDENT-LED TEACHER CONFERENCES

One way to support student agency is to offer "student-led" parent-teacher conferences. This approach revamps the old parent-teacher model and helps young people sharpen their communication skills and self-confidence.

This model allows students to be in the "driver's seat" and directly discuss growth and development—traditionally left to the adults. The practice helps students learn to articulate their needs and develop core competencies that will benefit them throughout their lives. And this isn't a new idea. Increasingly, middle and high school teachers nationwide are encouraging student-led parent conferences.

In 2016, the *Atlantic* documented the approach's effectiveness at a rural middle and high school in New Hampshire. Educators ditched the old teacher-led conference model after their school was rated one of the lowest performing in the state. Administrators and teachers knew certain practices needed to change if they wanted to improve student performance. Conferences were one of them.

Among the transition's positive outcomes, the school's conference participation jumped from less than 20% to over 90%. Students also expressed satisfaction with being included in discussions about their academic goals and progress (understandably so). But the shift from teacher-led to student-led wasn't just about boosting parental attendance or assignment grades. Giving students the opportunity to lead conferences gave them greater responsibility (Richmond, 2021).

If we're talking about student agency and giving our children greater control over their academic decisions, then we are also talking about increasing their responsibility. And to borrow a phrase from a beloved superhero, Spider-Man, with great power comes responsibility.

Teachers at that New Hampshire school not only wanted to guide young people on their academic journeys; they wanted to prepare them for life after school. Specifically, in life in the modern workplace, communication skills, self-direction, confidence, and the ability to take on bigger and more complicated tasks are keys to success.

These skills are vital in an era when young people are more inclined to text than speak—especially when engaging with strangers. And it's true, one of the most common challenges for teachers organizing student-led conferences is managing their student's nerves around presenting to an audience. It's especially tricky when their audience is family, and they're sharing strengths *and* weaknesses. Your sophomore won't just be showing off successful assignments.

Shyness is understandable. Parents' well-intended warnings about avoiding unfamiliar people led some youth to shun the natural and essential practice of confidence in communication and making new acquaintances. After all, deep friends typically begin their relationship as strangers. We build our capacity to trust in others by drawing comparisons from a vast range of encounters. Limited experience with strangers dampens our ability to make informed judgments.

Helping children overcome their apprehensions is in their best interests, and there are ways to alleviate that anxiety. Educational consultant

Ralinda Watts recommends engaging students in role-plays to ease tension before they lead their conferences. One-on-one coaching also helps students practice before the "big day" (Watts, 2022).

Students at the New Hampshire school began preparing for their conference a month in advance, staying organized with a checklist of items like selecting work samples and answering reflection prompts like "I'm really proud of (blank)" and "I still need help with (blank)." The conference preparation is itself beneficial for student development.

Student-led parent conferences can also encourage young people to engage more actively in the classroom. It integrates self-assessment into the learning process. Students develop a clearer understanding of the benchmarks that define their progress. They are also more likely to have suggestions about which additional supports might aid them.

Take Sarah Frayer, an award-winning educator who, as a child, went through the earlier part of grade school with undiagnosed dyslexia. "As I read, sometimes I couldn't make sense of combinations of words," she recalls. Without fully understanding why she struggled, Frayer intuitively asked for an audio device she could use to record herself reading text passages. The practice allowed her to playback sections at a more easily discernable pace. "My teacher was so impressed that I came up with a solution," she said.

Additionally, collaborating to construct an outline gives students a roadmap for what to expect. This might include discussing their academic strengths, areas for improvement, and any concerns or questions they may have. It's also essential to encourage their child to take ownership of their learning and express their thoughts and feelings respectfully and constructively.

You can help your child prepare by reviewing their work and progress together and practicing asking and answering questions. Additionally, you can encourage them to think about what they want to share with their teacher, such as goals for the school year or any accomplishments that are a source of pride. By involving your child in the conference process and helping them feel prepared, you can support their academic growth and foster a positive relationship with their teacher.

Students can cultivate a sense of self-directed learning when they lead conferences, even when they aren't meeting intended academic outcomes. Coach them to reframe "failures" as opportunities for growth. As previously referenced, researcher Carol Dweck had popularized the term *growth mindset* to describe how students benefit from viewing abilities as malleable rather than fixed. Having a growth mindset means understanding that temporary setbacks should be expected and are not insurmountable when learning. She describes the effort as a pathway to mastery (Dweck, 2006).

By cultivating a growth mindset in your child, you can help them approach challenges with a positive attitude and a willingness to learn and grow. One way to encourage a growth mindset is to praise effort, persistence, and strategies rather than solely focusing on outcomes or innate abilities. It's important to model a growth mindset by showing your child how you approach challenges, such as trying new things, embracing mistakes as opportunities for growth, and seeking feedback and support.

You can also encourage your child to set realistic goals and break them down into smaller steps, which can help them stay motivated and see progress over time. Additionally, you can help your child develop a sense of self-awareness by reflecting on their strengths and areas for improvement and setting new challenges to work toward. By fostering a growth mindset, you help your child develop resilience, persistence, and a lifelong love of learning.

Teacher-parent relations improve when there are touchpoints between formal meetings. Ask your child's teacher about their preferred mode for check-ins. This might include phone calls, emails, or even text messages. It's crucial to establish a regular communication routine that works for both the parent and the teacher and to respect each other's time and schedules.

TEACHING SELF-ADVOCACY

Parents who model respectful advocacy, as shared in stories throughout this book, go a long way toward preparing their children to follow their lead. It begins at an early age instilling in your child that they matter and their opinions have value.

Before and during much of the 20th century, children's perspectives were neither welcomed nor considered significant. In the "speak when you're spoken to" era, children weren't thought to have much to contribute—especially about their own affairs. A child's "job" was to follow instructions, get good grades, and fulfill their parents' ambitions. Historically, men were expected to inherit the family farm or trade, and women were to marry well and become docile homemakers. Or a male's job was to fulfill their father's unaccomplished vision—not your own.

Parents selected their children's spouses based on social standing, property ownership, and a male suitor's prospective ability to "provide" for his family. In communities of color, economic necessity dictated that both parents work. Still, when two parents were present, typical nuclear families were run as male-dominated households.

During the 1960s, students and young civil rights advocates dared question the dominant paradigm—and pushed back. Men rejected crew cuts, women demanded the right to work and fair pay, and students from all backgrounds refused to remain silent—resisting a failed war and the ills of racial segregation.

Decades later, globalization and the internet forever changed American domestic life and young people's worldviews. Models to live by were no longer restricted to experiences within local communities. Access to information was democratized, and lifestyle options previously unimaginable became possible. Young people gained easy access to distinctly different cultures, nontraditional family models, and unconventional career options. The "genie was out of the bottle," and public school systems still struggle to adapt and make sense of it all.

Similarly, students adversely impacted by gun violence and whose futures will be severely affected by climate change resoundingly declare they won't accept the status quo. Whether you consider the Parkland students' anti-gun advocacy or the *Black Lives Matter* movement, social activism is alive and well in ways we haven't seen since the 1960s and 1970s.

With much of the world's common knowledge accessible from one's handheld device, many students are rightfully questioning outdated modes of teaching and learning. Should they be expected to begin their career strapped with crippling debt from educational models that fail to inspire and lack imagination?

The lecture format, still prevalent at many of our college campuses, fails to engage and challenge students. Likewise, middle and high school students inherently understand that high-stakes tests don't adequately assess the totality of their knowledge or potential—and they are demanding more.

Our experiences during COVID-captivity taught us that learning need not be restricted to four walls or in person. Increasingly, the Netflix generation will insist on educational options that are flexible, on-demand, and convenient. Employers in many sectors are still trying to make sense of the "Great Resignation" or the "Big Quit" that accompanied COVID restrictions in 2021. Reliable workforces left their low-paying and uninspiring jobs en masse for less predictable but more fulfilling alternatives. Today's talented twentysomething who can is more inclined to insist on working remotely, and why not? Many are eager to become *digital nomads*, experiencing the world one Airbnb and new destination at a time.

Of course, employment flexibility is often limited to those with privilege. Service workers, many immigrants, may not easily afford such options. By necessity, a significant percentage of young people balance their school obligations with part-time employment, helping their families make ends meet. There are also "nontraditional" older students who must overcome learning gaps and beliefs that they don't belong.

Regardless of one's circumstances, complacency and accepting business as usual is no longer an option. Students can and must learn to advocate for themselves.

There comes a day when you say, "Enough." Abuse and addiction sufferers speak about reaching their "bottom"—a turning point when pain and suffering are no longer bearable. They emerge from the darkness, summoning an inner sense of strength that compels them to change. While comparisons are not proportional, watching your child suffer from educational experiences that visibly diminish their spirit and sense of self is painful.

That's why we need to begin measuring student achievement beyond academic progress. We need to think holistically and consider the entirety of a child's experience in the classroom. Educational organizations like the Association for Supervision and Curriculum Development (ASCD) have recently promoted the "Whole Child" approach as a way to foster student success beyond school, focusing on measures around health, safety, and engagement—not just grades (ASCD, n.d.).

Building on that work, we need to include agency in whole child assessment and underscore parental and self-advocacy as key factors in student success. It means honoring student voice and inviting students to make choices.

KEY TAKEAWAYS

This chapter explored how teachers and parents can work together and inspire their students to be active "co-designers" of their education. For a wide variety of reasons, many parents realize early on the need and the power of taking an active role in their child's education, from making sure their student is making progress in class, to ensuring they're being treated fairly. One effective way to rethink the parent-teacher relationship is through a reworking of the parent-teacher conference. Parents can make these meetings productive by arriving prepared with questions and ready to give teachers the benefit of the doubt, if they have concerns. Making these conferences student-led, elevates your child from a passive observer to a confident self-advocate, capable of making their own informed academic choices.

QUESTIONS TO CONSIDER

- What opportunities do you have to interact with your child's teachers? Do you have access to classroom materials?
- How do you prepare for conferences with your child's teacher?
- Does your child have opportunites to express their questions and concerns during parent-teacher conferences? Do they feel like they have a "seat at the table"?

REFERENCES

ASCD. (n.d.). *The whole child approach to education.* Retrieved March 25, 2023, from https://www.ascd.org/whole-child.

Dweck, Carol S. *Mindset: The new psychology of success.* Random house, 2006.

Richmond, E. (2021, May 4). *Should kids lead parent-teacher conferences? The Atlantic.* Retrieved March 25, 2023, from https://www.theatlantic.com/education/archive/2016/04/when-students-lead-parent-teacher-conferences/477069/

Sparks, S. D. (2020, December 1). *Parent-teacher conferences get a makeover. Education Week.* Retrieved March 25, 2023, from https://www.edweek.org/leadership/parent-teacher-conferences-get-a-makeover/2015/09

Watts, R. (2022, December 14). *Building student leadership skills through participation in parent-teacher conferences.* Edutopia. Retrieved March 25, 2023, from https://www.edutopia.org/article/student-led-parent-teacher-conferences/

Chapter 5

The Confidence Conundrum

When I lead university classes that include as many as 400 first-year undergraduates, I startle them with a career tip few expect to hear.

"Talk to strangers," I urge them, as a key personal and professional growth strategy. Not surprisingly, their responses range from expressions of horror to comical disbelief. It is easy to understand why.

Through films, books, and public service announcements, we've successfully instilled concerns about "stranger danger" in several generations of youth—but I argue it is to their detriment.

Youth abduction fears skyrocketed during the 1980s and 1990s, mostly due to media headlines rather than factual cases. According to the U.S. Department of Justice, most missing children are runaways, and relatives are responsible for 99% of child abductions (Finelhor & Hotaling, 1990).

My simple words of advice ring true. Building professional networks and spheres of influence requires engaging with unfamiliar people. Befriending strangers can be key to our growth. They can expose us to new ideas and unimagined opportunities. According to HubSpot, 85% of jobs are filled due to networking. CNBC asserts that 70% of all job openings are not published, and as many as 80% are found through personal and professional connections (Chang, 2023).

More so, engaging with strangers helps us develop our own sense of self. We clarify our own beliefs and values in comparison to others. In a word, we cultivate our sense of *confidence*.

Helping kids develop confidence is critical in this ever-challenging era. Geopolitical instability, global pandemics, climate change, and gun violence are legitimate threats that challenge young people's well-being and sanity. It stands to reason that 7 in 10 teens report struggling with mental health following COVID-19. More than half surveyed stated that the pandemic increased feelings of loneliness (National 4-H Council, 2020).

Confidence, in this context, refers to supporting youth to nurture a strong sense of self-assurance, self-worth, and trust in their abilities, skills, and judgments. It involves cultivating emotional resilience, enabling them to face challenges, take risks, and bounce back from setbacks with a positive attitude.

Fostering confidence begins at home by ensuring it is a safe and nurturing space where children feel comfortable expressing their thoughts, feelings, and emotions. That aim is not always easy for parents and guardians who face domestic challenges. Nearly 35%–50% of U.S. first-time marriages end in divorce (World Population Review, 2022) and nearly 24 million children live in single-parent families (Annie E. Casey Foundation, 2022). This isn't to suggest that single parents or guardians aren't great caregivers. Harmonious homes with nurturing single parents or guardians are preferable to traditional households dominated by domestic tension. Put simply, a loving household is the prime predictor of how children will develop and prosper.

Domestic strife and instability foster fear rather than confidence. For some children, school can become a safe haven—away from stressors at home. It may be a welcome refuge from parents who argue, abuse substances, or perpetrate neglect. Food insecurities and poor sleep habits may also inhibit students' learning abilities. More than 11 million U.S. children live below the federal poverty line, according to the National Center for Children in Poverty (United Way, 2023). Students suffering from hunger are more likely to score lower on standardized tests, repeat a grade, be suspended, get sick, and be hospitalized more frequently than their well-nourished peers (No Kid Hungry, n.d.). Families with means can take these basic needs for granted.

We develop children's confidence by modeling confident and respectful communication. Indeed, open communication flourishes through actively listening, empathizing, and validating your child's experiences. Encourage them to share their concerns and challenges and provide guidance without being overly critical or dismissive.

Students also can be inspired by peers. An example is Malala Yousafzai, a Pakistani activist for female education who demonstrated remarkable confidence in the face of adversity. After being targeted and shot by the Taliban for advocating girls' education, Malala continued her fight, becoming the youngest-ever Nobel Prize laureate at 17. "We realize the importance of our voices only when we are silenced," she states in *I am Malala*, the book that chronicles her story (Yousafzai, 2021). Malala's confidence in her beliefs and resilience has significantly impacted global education advocacy, inspiring countless others to join her cause.

Another example is Greta Thunberg, a Swedish environmental activist who gained international recognition for her efforts to combat climate change. At just 15 years old, Greta began protesting outside the Swedish parliament, demanding stronger action against the global crisis. Her confidence and determination to make a difference inspired millions of young people worldwide to join her in the "Fridays for Future" movement. "You are never too small to make a difference," she is quoted as saying (Kraemer, 2021). Greta's unwavering confidence enabled her to address world leaders at the United Nations Climate Action Summit and the World Economic Forum, driving positive change and sparking global conversations about climate change.

A third example is Easton LaChappelle, a high school student who developed a 3D-printed prosthetic arm controlled by brainwaves. His confidence and curiosity led him to learn about engineering, robotics, and programming through online resources, ultimately creating a low-cost, advanced prosthetic limb. Easton's innovative design caught the attention of NASA, and he later secured a position as a robotics engineer at the space agency (Elkins, 2018). His confidence in his abilities and his passion for learning enabled him to make a significant impact in the world of prosthetics.

These accomplishments may seem out-of-reach to young people with more humble aims. However, grassroots efforts in developing countries are just as evident. Xiuhtezcatl Martinez is an indigenous environmental activist from Colorado who began his journey as a grassroots organizer when he was just 6 years old. He has since mobilized young people around the world to fight for climate justice through his work with Earth Guardians, an organization that trains and supports young environmental activists. Martinez's confidence and passion for environmental justice have led him to address the United Nations General Assembly. "We felt as though we had a responsibility to do something about it. So, we did," Martinez says in *We Rise*, his co-authored book, designed to inspire other young people to take action in their communities. "The biggest issue we face is shifting human consciousness, not saving the planet. The planet does not need saving, we do" (Loftus-Farren, 2017).

Advocacy skills can be developed in one's neighborhood. Collecting canned goods door-to-door for local foodbanks, gathering Toys for Tots, or volunteering at one's area animal humane society—it all makes a difference and empowers young people to discover their ability to effect change.

ENCOURAGE PUBLIC SPEAKING

According to the National Institutes of Mental Health, 75% of individuals surveyed fear public speaking more than death. "Glossophobia" is the scientific word for fear of public speaking, originating from the Greek words "glossa" (tongue) and "phobos" (dread or fear). Such concerns stem from fear of being judged, failure, or simply lack of experience speaking publicly (LaDoucer, 2013).

However, the benefits of learning to speak publicly with confidence far outweigh the consequences of avoidance. Strong speaking skills can significantly and positively affect their academic and professional lives. For students, proficiency in speaking can lead to better grades, stronger critical thinking abilities, and increased participation in class discussions.

As young people learn to communicate their thoughts and ideas effectively, they begin to develop self-assurance and confidence in their abilities. Overcoming the fear of public speaking and becoming comfortable in front of an audience can empower them to tackle other challenges and take risks in various aspects of their lives.

As someone who presents to large groups of students on a regular basis, I can attest to the fact that it is perfectly natural to feel a sense of unease before addressing a group for the first time. I take it in stride, with an overall sense that my presentations will go well.

Public speaking is also an essential skill for aspiring leaders. By learning to articulate their thoughts and influence others, young people can hone their leadership abilities and effectively collaborate with peers. Effective communication skills enable future leaders to inspire, motivate, and engage with their teams, fostering a positive and productive work environment.

The professional world also highly values strong public speaking skills. Many careers require effective communication in meetings, presentations, and negotiations. By developing these skills early, young people can enhance their job prospects and excel in their chosen careers. Public speaking abilities can set them apart from their peers and open doors to new opportunities.

Here are some practical strategies:

1. Master the Basics: First and foremost, young speakers should familiarize themselves with the fundamental elements of public speaking. This includes maintaining proper posture, projecting their voice, making eye contact, and using appropriate gestures. Eye contact is particularly important. A good tip is for speakers to focus their gaze on three to four individuals throughout the room to make eye connect with. They'll soon notice nods and gestures that indicate their message is resonating, which bolsters confidence. By mastering these basics, new speakers can create a strong foundation to build their skills and develop a polished presentation style.
2. Prepare Thoroughly: One of the best ways to build confidence and deliver an engaging presentation is through thorough preparation. Encourage young speakers to research their topic extensively, organize their thoughts, and create an outline to guide their presentation. Working from an outline or a list of bullet points is preferable to rote memorization. This method comes across more naturally, and engenders deeper trust. Rehearsing a talk multiple times helps in becoming more comfortable with the material and identifying potential improvement areas.
3. Embrace Storytelling: Storytelling is a powerful tool to help young speakers connect with their audience and make their message more memorable. Encourage them to incorporate personal anecdotes, relevant examples, and vivid imagery to create a more engaging and relatable presentation. By using storytelling techniques, they can captivate their audience's attention and leave a lasting impression.

4. Practice Active Listening: To become effective communicators, young speakers should also develop their listening skills. Active listening involves fully concentrating, understanding, and responding to what others are saying. By practicing active listening, they can better understand their audience's needs, adapt their message accordingly, and create a more meaningful connection.
5. Learn from Others: Observing and learning from accomplished speakers can provide young people valuable insights and inspiration. Encourage them to watch speeches and presentations by skilled communicators, analyze their techniques, and incorporate those strategies into their own speaking style. Apple cofounder Steve Jobs was a masterful presenter. Suggest they search Youtube for "Steve Jobs iPhone product launch" to find the best examples. Former president Bill Clinton is another celebrated orator—and for good reason. Search "Clinton DNC convention speeches" for examples. Suggest that new speakers keep a journal while listening to great speakers to make note of tone, cadence, or intentional pauses that make for a great speech.
6. Join or Start a Public Speaking Club: Participating in a public speaking club or enrolling in a course can provide young people with a supportive environment to practice and refine their skills. Programs such as Toastmasters, debate clubs, or speech and drama classes can offer guidance, feedback, and opportunities to speak in front of an audience.
7. Seek Constructive Feedback: Constructive criticism is vital for growth and improvement. Young speakers should be encouraged to seek peer, teacher, or mentor feedback after their presentations. Recording practice sessions and actual presentations can help them identify strengths, recognize areas for improvement, and develop a more effective speaking style.
8. Cultivate a Growth Mindset: Developing strong public speaking skills takes time, effort, and persistence. By adopting a growth mindset, young people can view challenges and setbacks as opportunities for learning and growth. Encourage them to embrace mistakes, learn from their experiences, and continually strive to improve their skills.

PRACTICE BUILDS CONFIDENCE

It's common to falsely expect to be proficient at something without investing the time and energy necessary to attain mastery. In *Outliers*, author Malcolm Gladwell famously asserts that mastery requires 10,000 hours of practice (Gladwell, 2008). While Gladwell's claim has been debunked (Resnick, 2019) it is safe to say that commitment to practice is an essential aspect of improving one's abilities in most domains.

More so, young people experience growth when they set and achieve incremental milestones rather than tackle monumental goals. A common example is making a New Year's resolution to work out three times a week. Three times a week may be a tall order for someone beginning at zero. Better to commit to and accomplish a goal of working out twice a week before adding the third session.

When we fulfill our commitments and promises, it strengthens our confidence. We collect evidence that supports our progress. When we fail to fulfill our intentions, it breeds self-doubt and discontent.

This simple lesson is among the most significant we can instill in young people—the power of living as one's word. The world is listening when we declare an intention to achieve a future outcome. When we deliver, the reward is trust and high levels of opportunities. When we don't deliver, our words lack power, and others question our integrity.

KEY TAKEAWAYS

In this chapter, we explored the confidence conundrum facing students. Many young people today find even the prospect of approaching a stranger with a question to be anxiety inducing, let alone the idea of presenting a pitch to an audience of their peers. Fostering confidence at home and in school is key to raising empowered learners who are willing to take risks and refine their skills, and encouraging public speaking can build your child's confidence as well as develop their communication skills.

QUESTIONS TO CONSIDER

- How does your child feel about making class presentations? What do they do to prepare?
- Does your child participate in extracurricular activities? Do they volunteer? Does your child have opportunities to practice effective communications skills outside the classroom?
- What kind of communication do you model for your child at home? Does your child feel open to share their concerns or challenges at school?

REFERENCES

The Annie E. Casey Foundation. (2022, August 1). *Child well-being in single-parent families*. Retrieved April 12, 2023, from https://www.aecf.org/blog/child-well-being-in-single-parent-families

Chang, J. (2023, March 15). *85 crucial networking statistics you need to know in 2023*. Financesonline.com. Retrieved April 12, 2023, from https://financesonline.com/networking-statistics/

Elkins, K. (2018, December 5). *Meet the 23-year-old inventor Tony Robbins calls "the next Elon Musk."* CNBC. Retrieved April 12, 2023, from https://www.cnbc.com/2018/12/05/tony-robbins-23-year-old-easton-lachappelle-is-the-next-elon-musk.html

Finelhor, D., Hotaling, G., & Sedlak, A. (1990). *Missing, Abudcted, Runaway, and Thrownaway Children in America*. Office of Juvenile Justice and Delinquency Prevention.

Kraemer, D. (2021, November 5). *Greta Thunberg: Who is the climate campaigner and what are her aims?* BBC News. Retrieved April 12, 2023, from https://www.bbc.com/news/world-europe-49918719

LaDoucer, P. (2013, September 12). *What we fear more than death*. MentalHelp.net. Retrieved April 12, 2023, from https://www.mentalhelp.net/blogs/what-we-fear-more-than-death/

Loftus-Farren, Z. (2017). *Xiuhtezcatl Martinez. Earth Island Journal*. Retrieved April 12, 2023, from https://www.earthisland.org/journal/index.php/magazine/entry/xiuhtezcatl_martinez/

National 4-H Council. (2020, June 17). *New survey finds 7 in 10 teens are struggling with mental health*. PR Newswire: press release distribution, targeting, monitoring and marketing. Retrieved April 12, 2023, from https://www.prnewswire.com/news-releases/new-survey-finds-7-in-10-teens-are-struggling-with-mental-health-301078336.html

No Kid Hungry. (n.d.). *Learn how hunger affects your school.* Center for Best Practices—No Kid Hungry. Retrieved April 12, 2023, from http://bestpractices.nokidhungry.org/playbook/schools/learn-how-hunger

Resnick, B. (2019, August 23). *The "10,000-hour rule" was debunked again. That's a relief.* Vox. Retrieved April 12, 2023, from https://www.vox.com/science-and-health/2019/8/23/20828597/the-10000-hour-rule-debunked

United Way NCA. (2023, March 22). *Child poverty in America—Facts, statistics.* Retrieved April 12, 2023, from https://unitedwaynca.org/blog/child-poverty-in-america/

World Population Review. (n.d.). *Divorce Rate by State 2023.* Retrieved April 12, 2023, from https://worldpopulationreview.com/state-rankings/divorce-rate-by-state

Yousafzai, M. (2021). *Biography.* A&E Television. Retrieved April 12, 2023, from https://www.biography.com/activists/malala-yousafzai

Chapter 6

Voice and Choice

Building upon the previous chapter, *voice,* and *choice* are operative words that empower students and "flip the switch." In this chapter, I address ways of activating student voice and sharing power to encourage genuine choice. When cultivated, students discover an ability to initiate and cocreate assignments that challenge their current level of understanding and propel their growth. They take ownership and responsibility for their place in the classroom and the world.

When JLI cofounder Esther Wojcicki inherited Palo Alto High School's *Campanile* newspaper in 1984, just a dozen students were engaged in the fledging program. By the time she retired in 2021, over 800 participated and produced more than a dozen student-run publications. She created a complete culture shift on campus. Journalism emerged as the "must do" popular program.

How and why? A bit of history is in order. I first discovered Esther and her program in 2010 while searching for a dissertation topic. We met at a conference, where she arrived with three of her students in tow. Within minutes, it was evident; these were no average high school students. They were poised, professional, and incredibly curious. I learned that the program led the nation in prestigious student press awards and was among the nation's largest. The more we talked, the more I became convinced that my search for a topic had ended.

My earliest suspicion was that perhaps the results I witnessed were attributable to privilege, given the community's high level of affluence. The high school is across the street from Stanford, and Google and Facebook headquarters are nearby.

However, the more I researched, the more it became apparent that the magic at "Paly" (as locals call it) could be replicated in community schools with far less wealth. I spent the next 2 years making about a dozen pilgrimages to Palo Alto to observe and video record the program in action. I witnessed pedagogical practices that were anything but orthodox. At *Campanile* newspaper meetings, a team of five or more student-selected editors led instruction from the front of the room while Esther sat at her desk at the back. The students were clearly in charge.

Journalism students at Paly weren't forced-fed what teachers thought they needed to know. Nearly every aspect of the program was student-generated, from story assignments to copyediting. During production weeks, students stayed late into the evenings to make deadlines.

Recruiting future journalists was never the program's aim. Earlier on, Wojcicki, Paul Kandell, and their teaching team recognized that journalism offers students critical skills needed to succeed in the information era. In this new era, we change employers more frequently than in years past, placing higher consideration and demands on how, when, and where we work.

The "Lone Ranger" work ethos is a sentiment of the past. Corporate employees are more likely to work collaboratively than alone in offices or cubicles. Indeed, many of today's workspaces resemble newsrooms, with coworkers floating from one area to another.

Upon completing my dissertation and doctoral program, Esther and I joined forces. We formed a nonprofit organization that became the Journalistic Learning Initiative, with financial support from philanthropist Tara Guber and from the University of Oregon donors Nancy and Dave Petrone.

In 2016, we piloted our work at a rural middle school in Western Oregon, an area that was hit hard economically by a decline in the timber industry. We launched in a conservative-voting community as a newly elected Trump administration fueled doubt and disagreement about the journalism profession—questioning its ethics and integrity. We received zero pushback and encountered no controversies, which we attributed to our conviction to stay above the fray of politicized issues.

Sixth-grade students amazed us with their depth of courage and conviction. After all, journalistic tasks may seem too rigorous for sixth graders to take on, at least at first glance. Ages 11 and 12 are more inclined to text their friends than call them. They are also raised to avoid strangers. Consequently, social skills older adults take for granted are more challenging for pre-teenagers. Adolescence is already an awkward stage of life. Growth spurts, acne, braces, and hormonal imbalances add to the difficulties many of us dreaded as middle school students. Journalistic learning challenges students to step beyond what's familiar. They learn the value of engaging with new people and topics and how to collaborate with peers.

It was strikingly apparent that young people thrive and emerge as self-determined learners when their intrinsic interests are honored. They are granted permission to select assignments aligned with those interests. Students engaged in topics such as homelessness, animal cruelty, and veterans' rights.

An example is Taylor, whose group focused on homelessness. Before the project, he believed that most homeless people's plight was attributable to laziness and a desire to bilk the system. However, his eyes were opened after engaging with the director of a local homeless shelter.

"Many of our clients are children your age or younger," she said. "Sometimes their parents have experienced a catastrophic illness inadequately covered by health insurance, or they lost their job during the economic crisis. Despite their sincere effort, they may encounter difficulty securing new employment."

Another example is Todd, a biracial student whose team examined racism. Their internet research uncovered unsettling websites intending to inspire hate. Todd said: "When you're growing up, you think of racism being in the past—Martin Luther King, Jr. . . . You don't consider the newer forms."

The experience inspired Todd to grow his hair long as an affirmation of pride in his heritage. "I saw a picture of my dad as a teenager with an Afro," Todd said. "He's bald now, so I never pictured him with hair. I thought, why not? So I grew my hair out."

Both students shared lasting impressions of participating 2 years after the pilot program. "My opinions were quite strong back then," Taylor said. "I learned that public assistance can actually help some people get back on their feet."

Participating students learned to question their assumptions and to ground their assertions in verifiable evidence. Additionally, they discovered that it is okay to have strong opinions as long as you express them respectfully. Divisive politics leaves young people bereft of public figures who can serve as positive role models for appropriate ways to engage with one another. We continue to visit with many of those pilot-year students as they prepare to finish high school and enter college.

Nearly a decade later, the program has grown to serve nearly 10,000 middle and high school students in five states and is on its way to nationwide expansion. The evolution of JLI's work is represented in our *Effective Communicators* program, instructional materials that teachers implement as a 10-week unit over their English language arts curriculums. The program acknowledges that communication skills are critical in every aspect of life. Whether interviewing for employment, making a public presentation, or negotiating the purchase price for a car, one's ability to effectively speak, write, and engage with others is essential. While students practice these skills across the curriculum, *Effective Communicators* adds additional emphasis.

In groups of three or four, students select community concerns that align with their intrinsic interests. They research, identify and interview experts, write articles, and then publish their work online, where friends, family, and community members can view it. They're not just writing a project for a grade; they're writing for an audience.

For many students, that's what gives journalistic learning its punch. The news articles students produce focus on real-world topics that matter to people and, importantly, matter to them. They're topics they want to research, discuss, and write about.

"I think it's good because we're focusing on current things as well as future things," said Mai, a student at Adrienne Nelson High School in Happy Valley, Oregon, one of the schools that's used the Effective Communicators program in their English Language Arts classrooms.

Mai's group wrote about abortion, an issue that gripped the nation and dominated the headlines last year after the Supreme Court overturned the landmark Roe vs. Wade decision. For Mai, past English classes were all about the mechanics of the five-paragraph essay and following the textbook. But with this course, she could explore (and localize) her interest in a national story relevant to her life and the lives of her peers.

Writing for publication, not a teacher's grade, was one of the few ways she could channel that curiosity. "I'm still young, and I know I can't really do much except put my voice out there," Mai said.

You don't have to reside in a state where JLI's work is prevalent to have your child benefit from our educational philosophies. Educators across the United States are being invited to participate. Additionally, JLI is developing a self-guided version of its Effective Communicator program that students can access for credit recovery and after-school exploration. For more information, visit journalisticlearning.org.

KEY TAKEAWAYS

This chapter explored the benefits of giving students voice and choice—in this case, through *journalistic learning*. This project-based storytelling approach to English language arts class has students form groups and collaborate on news stories about issues that matter to them. Students emerge from this process as empowered, self-directed learners, who choose their own topics of interest and write stories for an audience of their family, their peers, and their community. Students aren't just writing for a grade.

QUESTIONS TO CONSIDER

- What news stories grab your child's attention? What topics are they interested in exploring or writing about?
- How often does your child get to choose topics for their own writing assignments at school?
- How does your child feel about working in groups? Do they often have opportunities to collaborate on projects?

Chapter 7

Amplification

At age 12, I launched a neighborhood newspaper. More accurately, I created a one-sheet handout using an old mimeograph duplicating machine my mom brought home from the school where she taught. For the unfamiliar, the mid-20th-century devices worked by transferring ink onto paper through a stencil created from an original document or image. Once created, the stencil was attached to the machine's drum, which rotated as the paper fed through. The smell of the paper copies was distinctly indelible, a potent mix of alcohol-based solvents that probably would be deemed unsafe for school use today.

The project provided opportunities to improve my writing and taught me the importance of meeting deadlines. Also, it gave me an authentic audience. Distributing it door-to-door taught me to engage with neighbors and learn about community concerns. I was awestruck by the realization that my neophyte reporting was cultivating a following.

Throughout history, publishing has played a decisive role in shaping ideas, movements, and societies. From the earliest forms of written communication, such as hieroglyphics and cuneiform, publishing has enabled people to share their ideas and knowledge with a broader audience.

During the Enlightenment period in the 18th century, publishing played a crucial role in disseminating new scientific and philosophical ideas. Writers such as Voltaire and Rousseau used their works to challenge traditional beliefs and advocate for freedom of thought and expression. Gutenberg's printing press forever democratized knowledge. It liberated peasants from the church's sole authority and fueled literacy throughout Europe. Similarly, the internet, YouTube, blogging, and podcasts have democratized "mainstream" media. The barrier to entry for publishing has never been lower.

However, it's important for young writers to learn that the power to publish comes with responsibility. We've experienced the repercussions when misinformation gains currency. For instance, during the COVID-19 pandemic, numerous false claims and conspiracy theories were circulating on social media and other online platforms. Some people believed that the virus was a hoax, that masks were ineffective or even harmful, and that unproven treatments like hydroxychloroquine were beneficial. Such misinformation not only put individuals at risk, but also had the potential to undermine public health efforts to control the spread of the virus.

We've also witnessed how false information can be spread to manipulate public opinion, leading to increased polarization and division within society. In some cases, this can even lead to violence and social unrest, as seen in the spread of false information during elections or political protests. The starkest example occurred on January 6, 2021, when a mob of former president Donald Trump supporters stormed the U.S. Capitol. Misinformation and conspiracy theories about the 2020 presidential election being "stolen" from Trump significantly fueled the riot.

False narratives have also fueled political tension internationally. In 2007, false rumors and fake news spread on social media and other online platforms and fueled violence and riots following the presidential election in Kenya. More than 1,000 people were killed, and hundreds of thousands were displaced.

Publishing is *journalistic learning*'s "secret weapon." It's what distinguishes it from other pedagogical approaches. Sharing one's work with a broader audience than one's teacher makes it a "real" and worthy experience. Students bring their "A" game to the process, realizing that their peers, parents, and community will view their work. They also discover that words and images have the power—to influence others and inspire change. Several examples underscore how students have used the power of the press for public benefit.

Following the mass shooting at Marjory Stoneman Douglas High School in Parkland, Florida, in 2018, student journalists at the school's newspaper, *The Eagle Eye*, played a crucial role in keeping the public informed about the tragedy and its aftermath. Student journalists were on the front lines of the crisis, and their reporting gave voice to the students and families affected by the tragedy. They interviewed survivors, witnesses, and family members of the victims, providing a more personal and emotional perspective than traditional news outlets.

"It was kind of hard to find students who were OK with speaking," Parkland student journalist Christy Ma told NPR one week after the tragedy. "It was hard to [report] objectively, as we were survivors of this incident" (Lombardo, 2018).

They also investigated the shooter's history and law enforcement's failures to prevent the shooting, holding those in power accountable for their actions.

In addition to their reporting, the student journalists became vocal advocates for gun control, leading a national movement for stricter gun laws. They organized protests and rallies, spoke at national events, and used their platform to demand change.

A week after the tragedy, dozens of students traveled to the state capital in Tallahassee to lobby for a ban on assault-style rifles. Waves and applause greeted them from fellow teens. "We're here to make sure this never happens again," said Diego Pfeiffer, a senior at Stoneman (Powell, 2018). Their efforts helped to bring the issue of gun violence to the forefront of the national conversation and sparked a renewed debate about gun control laws.

The Parkland student journalists were recognized for their work, receiving numerous awards and accolades, including the Pulitzer Prize for their shooting coverage. Their reporting and advocacy demonstrated the power of student journalism to make a difference and influence public opinion on important social and political issues.

In another example, student reporters at *The Harbinger*, the student newspaper at Shawnee Mission East High School in Kansas, investigated the school district's administration of student fees. Their reporting uncovered discrepancies and led to changes in how the district handles these fees, demonstrating the ability of student journalism to hold those in power accountable and bring about change.

The student reporters began their investigation by investigating the fees for participating in extracurricular activities, such as sports and clubs. They found that the district was not following its own policies regarding these fees, leading to confusion and inequities among students.

Through public records requests and interviews with school officials and parents, the student journalists uncovered a number of discrepancies in the way the district handled student fees. For example, some students were being charged fees that were higher than what the district had approved, while others were being charged for activities that were supposed to be free.

The student reporters published their findings in a series of articles in *The Harbinger*, bringing attention to the issue and sparking a public debate. Their reporting led to changes in how the district handles student fees, with the district implementing new policies to ensure that fees are applied fairly and consistently district-wide.

The Harbinger's investigation also received national recognition, winning a number of awards, including the Columbia Scholastic Press Association's Gold Crown Award and the National Scholastic Press Association's Pacemaker Award.

The student journalists at *The Harbinger* demonstrated the power of investigative reporting and student journalism's impact in holding those in power accountable. Their reporting brought about real change in their community and serves as an inspiration to student journalists everywhere.

STUDENT RIGHTS AND FIRST AMENDMENT

Civics lessons introduce students to the First Amendment and rights related to self-expression. The *Tinker v. Des Moines Independent Community School District* case, which the U.S. Supreme Court decided in 1969, remains a landmark decision in America's history of free speech and student rights.

The case arose from a protest by students at a Des Moines, Iowa, high school wearing black armbands to protest the Vietnam War. The school district had banned wearing armbands, citing concerns that the protest would disrupt the educational environment.

The students, represented by the American Civil Liberties Union (ACLU), sued the school district, arguing that their First Amendment rights to free speech and expression had been violated. The case eventually made its way to the Supreme Court, which ruled in favor of the students in a 7–2 decision.

The *Tinker* decision established an important precedent for the rights of students in public schools. The Court held that students do not "shed their constitutional rights to freedom of speech or expression at the schoolhouse gate," and that schools may only regulate student speech if it "materially and substantially disrupts" the educational process.

The Court's decision significantly impacted the rights of students in public schools, protecting their right to express their opinions and beliefs without fear of censorship or retaliation. The decision also helped to establish the importance of student activism and protest in our democracy, recognizing that young people have an essential role to play in shaping public opinion and driving social change.

However, in the decades since *Tinker*, there have been numerous challenges to students' free speech rights, and the interpretation of the decision has been debated and refined in subsequent cases. Two decades later, the Supreme Court backtracked its stance in a case that directly affected student journalism.

In 1988, the *Hazelwood School District v. Kuhlmeier* case involved the school district's censorship of a high school newspaper and significantly impacted student journalists' rights in the United States. The case began in 1983 when the principal of Hazelwood East High School in Missouri, Robert Reynolds, deleted two articles from the school newspaper, *The Spectrum*, without the knowledge or consent of the student journalists who had written them. The articles covered sensitive topics, including teen pregnancy and the impact of divorce on students, and included interviews with students who had shared their personal experiences (U.S. Courts, n.d).

The student journalists were outraged by the censorship and filed a lawsuit against the school district, arguing that their First Amendment rights had been violated. The case eventually made its way to the Supreme Court, which ruled in favor of the school district in a 5–3 decision.

The ruling stated that school officials can exercise "editorial control" over school-sponsored publications if their actions are "reasonably related to legitimate pedagogical concerns." The Court argued that the articles in question were sensitive and potentially harmful to the students involved and that the principal's decision to censor them was justified. The ruling led to increased awareness of the importance of a free and independent student press, and it sparked a national debate about the role of student journalism in schools.

In response to the *Hazelwood* decision, guided by the Student Press Law Center's Model Act for Student Expression, nearly 20 states have enacted laws to protect the rights of student journalists. These laws protect the rights of student journalists to express their opinions and report on issues of public concern without fear of censorship or retaliation.

The *Hazelwood* case remains a landmark decision in the history of student journalism and a reminder of the importance of protecting students' First Amendment rights. It also serves as a testament to the power of student journalism to hold those in power accountable and to bring about positive change in our society.

RETHINKING TRADITIONAL WRITING ASSIGNMENTS

Teaching the traditional five-paragraph essay format has long been a staple of writing instruction in American schools. Still, many educators and writing experts now argue that this approach is passé and ineffective. Instead, they advocate for a more journalistic writing instruction approach focusing on real-world writing skills and techniques.

One of the primary reasons why the five-paragraph essay format is seen as outdated is that it does not reflect the real-world writing situations that students are likely to encounter outside the classroom. In journalism, for example, writers must be able to write clearly, concisely, and effectively, often under tight deadlines and with limited space. This requires a different set of skills than those needed to write a formulaic essay that follows a strict structure.

Another reason the format is seen as passé is that it does not encourage creativity or critical thinking. By focusing on a rigid structure and formula, students may feel constrained in their writing and may not be encouraged to explore new ideas or take risks with their writing. In contrast, journalistic writing encourages writers to be creative and think critically about the topics they cover, often requiring them to analyze complex issues and present them clearly and engagingly.

Finally, the five-paragraph essay format may not prepare students for the types of writing they will be expected to do in college and beyond.

In many college classes, for example, students will be expected to write research papers, persuasive essays, and other types of writing that require more sophisticated writing skills and techniques. Journalistic assignments teach students to gather, synthesize, and concisely convey information to be understood. These vital skills can benefit them across disciplines as they prepare for college and their careers.

But what if your child's school doesn't offer instruction informed by a journalistic lens? You and other parents can initiate the concept by researching the topic further and sharing the benefits. Point teachers and administrators to the Journalistic Learning Initiative's website: http://journalisticlearning.org, featuring videos of the approach in action. The JLI Educator program also offers teachers online training and support. Additionally, this and our team's previous books provide educators with numerous resources.

Students no longer need a toxic and cumbersome printing device to experience the power of publishing for an audience. Blogging platforms now allow anyone with internet access and a keyboard to practice reporting. With just a few clicks, anyone can set up a blog and start sharing their thoughts, ideas, and experiences with the world.

Digital publishing has revolutionized the world of journalistic expression, providing numerous benefits over traditional print publishing, including reaching a wider global audience. Another benefit is incorporating multimedia elements into stories, such as photos, videos, and interactive graphics. This allows for a more immersive and engaging reading experience and bring stories to life in ways that are impossible with print publishing. Digital publishing also allows for greater flexibility in content distribution, with articles and stories able to be shared across various platforms and channels.

An example is JLI's Black Student Magazine project (http://blackstudentmagazine.com), created by and for middle and high school students nationwide. Intended for all audiences, the academic enrichment program also fosters cultural pride. Student contributors meet weekly via Zoom, where they engage with prominent guest speakers before moving into breakout sessions where Black undergraduate journalism students provide research and writing support. The annual publication reaches after-school program students in 93 cities through a partnership with the National Urban League.

As exemplified throughout this book, a shift occurs when young people are offered opportunities to explore and write about topics that align with their intrinsic interests. Writing assignments are no longer perceived as a chore. Rather, they become an opportunity to investigate and share one's curiosities, interests, and passions.

If your child struggles with traditional writing assignments, ask their teacher whether journalistic strategies can be used to achieve the same learning objectives. Can assignments be tied to something your child genuinely cares about or their lived experiences? Is there an opportunity to engage in deeper research? Might they interview individuals who would expand their perspectives? Finally, might there be an opportunity for your child to publish their work for a wider audience?

JLI has also developed online tools that give students parent-supervised self-guided opportunities to benefit from the journalistic learning approach. The organization makes the tools available to individuals and after-school programs.

KEY TAKEAWAYS

In this chapter, we explored how amplification can transform children from passive students into empowered learners who consider the impact of their voice. The act of publishing, whether it's a new book, news story, or a social media post, can help shape movements, change public opinion, and shine a light on forgotten issues. In recent history, the published work of student journalists has not only helped hold office holders accountable, but also helped define and protect the rights of student expression.

QUESTIONS TO CONSIDER

- How does your child interact with social media? What kind of content do they share?
- What does your child think about their role in the community? What responsibilities do they have?
- Does your child struggle with the five-paragraph essay?

REFERENCES

Lombardo, C. (2018, February 22). *"It's not just a story. it's our lives": Student journalists in Parkland.* NPR. Retrieved March 25, 2023, from https://www.npr.org/sections/ed/2018/02/22/587754623/student-journalists-at-marjory-stoneman-douglas-it-s-not-just-a-story-it-s-our-l

Powell, T. (2018, February 21). *Tearful Florida school students arrive in state capital for rally.* Evening Standard. Retrieved March 25, 2023, from https://www.standard.co.uk/news/world/florida-school-shooting-tearful-students-arrive-in-state-capital-gun-control-rally-a3771776.html

U.S. Courts. (n.d.). *Facts and case summary—Hazelwood v. Kuhlmeier.* Retrieved March 25, 2023, from https://www.uscourts.gov/educational-resources/educational-activities/facts-and-case-summary-hazelwood-v-kuhlmeier

Chapter 8

Advocating for Children with Special Needs

Our communities have significant numbers of young people who have difficulty advocating for themselves in ways their peers may take for granted. As a society, we've come a long way in discussing and including students with disabilities. Suspecting and later confirming that your child may have special needs is its own hero's journey for ill-prepared parents who make very emotional decisions about what's best for their child.

For inexplicable reasons, the rate of children diagnosed with some form of autism has increased exponentially in the United States. It is estimated that autism affects over seven million American youth. In New York and New Jersey alone, the number of diagnoses tripled between 2000 and 2016. According to the Centers for Disease Control, 1 in 54 children had been diagnosed with autism by age 8 in 2016, compared to 1 in 150 in 2000 (NBC, 2023).

Parents who are new to navigating unexpected, related challenges can easily become overwhelmed. For my family, it is a personal matter. My younger sister Karyn and her husband were enjoying successful East Coast careers 2 years into their marriage. She worked in fashion merchandising for a top New York-based brand, and he worked as a computer engineer. They purchased their first home in a nearby New Jersey suburb and were eager to have their first child. However, within the 1st year of my nephew Matthew's birth, they became concerned.

"When he was 14 months old, I began noticing that he couldn't sit up, like support his trunk, in a high chair. So I placed a pillow on either side of him," Karyn recalled. An initial hunch foretold further unsettling discoveries. She knew, developmentally, something wasn't right.

"Also, the biggest thing was that he wasn't speaking." Based on these symptoms, their pediatrician ordered a blood test.

"They called us on the phone to tell us, which to me felt insensitive," she remembers. The results showed that Matthew tested positive for Fragile X syndrome, a genetic disorder within the autism spectrum that can adversely affect cognitive development.

"We had never heard of it," Karyn shared. "My first thought was, are we ever going to be happy again? Because it was such a blow." They began reading any and all available literature, trying to glean what Matthew's future and their family's prospects might be.

Two weeks into daycare services, Karyn received a concerned phone call from the providers about Matthew's socialization skills. "He wouldn't interact with the other children," she recalls. The care facility had an observation window. Karyn stood there with the staff, grasping why they had summoned her. The children were visibly playing together except Matthew, who had separated himself and rocked back and forth.

"It was the first time I thought, with my very own eyes, he's quite different," she said. Being parents with means allowed them to fly Matthew to UC Davis, in California, one of the leading research universities that study Fragile X. "They wanted to take his picture because they didn't have a lot of pictures of African-American kiddos," she recalled.

The researchers confirmed Matthew's diagnosis and informed Karyn that she was a genetic carrier. "They also informed us that if he didn't begin speaking by age seven, it was unlikely that he ever would," she said. Few words adequately described the flood of emotions they felt. Like many new parents who have faced similar news, they struggled to understand it all.

"Why us? Why our family?" were the internalized thoughts dominating their medical sessions. My sister recalls from our childhood that we were raised to believe in a punishing God. "Nothing bad had ever happened to me before," she said.

Their pastor counseled that they should view Matthew's innocence as a gift. "God can do more with him the way he is," the pastor said. "That resonated with me, and I love that he said that because when Matthew laughs, he laughs from a deep place."

With time, Karyn began to see the gifts from mothering Matthew. "He's pure in his behavior. There's no malice. When people encounter him, they quickly realize he's a person with challenges, and it has them reflect on their own lives."

As Matthew became school-age, Karyn reached out and found communities of parents facing similar concerns through local support groups and online forums. "I met other moms, and we had a special needs playgroup, sometimes with as many as 13 kiddos, all with different diagnoses." The moms shared strategies for navigating relationships with school administrators and teachers.

SPECIAL NEEDS AND PUBLIC SCHOOLS

In earlier eras, school districts educated students with disabilities separately from their peers. However, in recent decades various levels of "inclusion" have become the norm. Karyn learned that special needs diagnoses and behaviors typically fall into three categories. According to *Autism Parenting Magazine*, *level one* is the highest functioning category. It indicates that a child may need support but can develop a range of social skills and independence. Children categorized at *level two* have verbal, social, and behavioral deficits, even with support in place. *Level three* autism indicates the highest need for socializing, speaking, and communicating non-verbally (Hobbs, 2022).

"Severe needs children may not be independent with their toileting," Karyn said, which was the case with Matthew.

Regardless of the severity, the Individuals with Disabilities Education Act (IDEA) entitles every child to a "free and appropriate education." However, how the standard is defined and met differs depending on the state.

"A lot has to do with the school district you live in, in terms of what kind of support you're going to receive," said Betsy Ballard, a retired Pennsylvania teacher who continues to support parents in understanding and advocating for their rights. It is not uncommon for parents to move to a different county or state to access what's best for their child. However, families living in poverty do not enjoy such mobility.

Understanding your child's rights as they enter public school is essential to being able to advocate on their behalf. To access accommodations, parents must learn a host of acronyms and numbers that govern their relationship with the school district. "Often the gateway is something called an ISP, an Instructional Support Plan," Ballard said. "An instructional support team or teacher parses things out to figure out if the situation is something they can address by having intensive instruction, or should they go for something more intensive, which would be the 504 and leading into an IEP."

A 504 plan refers to Section 504 of the Rehabilitation Act of 1973. It is essentially the "blueprint" for how the school will remove learning barriers for your child. IEP is an Individualized Educational Plan developed to ensure your child receives specialized instruction and services.

IEPs are determined by your child's needs, not the school district's budget. Still, disparities are common.

Intending "full disclosure," a school staff member can hand parents a stack of documents filled with legalese that many administrators themselves don't understand. "Because IEPs are legally binding, some have turned into 40, 50, or 60-page documents," Ballard said.

Using the words "due process" commands a higher level of attention from a school district. It essentially is a threat to take the school district to court. "The minute that you say that at an IEP meeting, school districts can go one of two ways," Ballard said. "I've seen it go where they will fight a parent in court. But I've also seen students who didn't necessarily qualify given a free ride at the school of their choice." Rather than experience media and public shame, some districts will pay to provide a child with private education.

While there is little hard data (Langreo, 2022), students with special needs likely were more adversely affected by Covid-related learning loss than their peers. The sparse stats demonstrate how students with disabilities' concerns can frequently be overlooked.

"If we don't have a baseline understanding, we won't be able to understand recovery efforts, and we won't be able to understand what is effective in supporting students' recovery, and we won't also know where to target the most support," Laura Stelitano, a research manager for the Center for Learner Equity told Education Week.

EdWeek found that more states observed declining graduation rates for students with disabilities. In fact, according to their research, 22 states saw declining graduation rate among students with disabilities in 2020–2021, compared with 10 states the previous year (Sparks, 2022).

Ballard and my sister Karyn advise parents never to go it alone. Connect with and seek support from other parents when engaging with teachers, administrators, or district officials. Document everything, phone calls, emails, and meetings. You want to assemble a paper trail that outlines your requests and their responses.

As a parent of a special needs child, many resources are available to help you navigate the challenges of advocating for your child's education. Examples include:

1. Parent Training and Information Centers (PTIs)—PTIs provide information, training, and support to parents of children with disabilities. They can help you navigate the special education system and advocate for your child's needs. To find a PTI in your area, visit the Parent Technical Assistance Center Network website.
2. Council of Parent Attorneys and Advocates (COPAA)—COPAA is a national organization that provides legal assistance and advocacy support to parents of children with disabilities. They can help you understand your child's legal rights and advocate for appropriate services and accommodations.
3. National Center for Learning Disabilities (NCLD)—The NCLD is a nonprofit organization that provides information and resources for parents of children with learning disabilities. They offer a range of resources, including webinars, workshops, and publications, to help parents advocate for their children.
4. Understood.org—Understood.org is a comprehensive online resource for parents of children with learning and attention issues. They offer personalized resources, such as articles, videos, and tools, to help parents understand their child's needs and advocate for their education.
5. Special Education Resource Hubs—Many states have special education resource hubs that provide information and support to parents of children with disabilities. To find a hub in your state, visit the National Dissemination Center for Children with Disabilities website.

Staying informed and educated about your child's rights and the services and accommodations available is also essential. This may involve researching educational laws and regulations, attending workshops and conferences, and networking with other parents of special needs children. Finally, advocating for your child is a team effort. Work closely with your child's teachers, therapists, and other professionals to ensure that your child's needs are met. Be open to collaboration and willing to listen to the perspectives and insights of others. Following these tips can help ensure your child receives the support and accommodations they need to thrive.

KEY TAKEAWAYS

In this chapter, we explored ways parents and teachers can advocate for students wtih special needs. It can be overwhelming as a parent to navigate our complicated education system when rasing a child with special needs, especially when supports and policies vary from district to district. That's why understanding your child's rights and staying informed about the services available to them is critical. But it's also important to remember you're not alone in this process. Advocating for your child is a team effort and teachers can prove to be strong allies.

QUESTIONS TO CONSIDER

- Does your child need extra support in the classroom? Do they struggle with certain assignments?
- What kind of supports and services are available at your child's school? How accessible are those supports?
- Do you connect with other parents whose children have similar struggles? What's your support network look like?

REFERENCES

Hobbs, K. (2022, January 6). *Severe Low Functioning Autism—What sets it apart*. Autism Parenting. Retrieved March 25, 2023, from https://www.autismparentingmagazine.com/low-functioning-autism/#the-three-levels-of-autism

Langreo, L. (2022, October 24). There's little data on the pandemic's effect on students with disabilities. that's a big problem. *Education Week*. Retrieved

March 25, 2023, from https://www.edweek.org/teaching-learning/theres-little-data-on-the-pandemics-effect-on-students-with-disabilities-thats-a-big-problem/2022/10

NBCUniversal News Group. (2023, January 26). *Autism rates have tripled. is it more common or are we better at diagnosis?* NBCNews.com. Retrieved March 25, 2023, from https://www.nbcnews.com/health/health-news/autism-rates-rising-more-prevalent-versus-more-screening-rcna67408

Sparks, S. D. (2022, September 6). Plunging graduation rates signal long recovery. *Education Week.* Retrieved March 25, 2023, from https://www.edweek.org/teaching-learning/plunging-graduation-rates-signal-long-recovery/2022/08

Chapter 9

Your Child's First Teacher

"Parents are a child's first teacher," says Celeste, an early childhood development specialist who taught preschool in the Washington DC metro area. Early in her career, Celeste developed a reputation as a teacher with a gift for connecting with preschool children and bringing forth their greatness, to many parents' pleasant surprise.

"At the beginning of the school year, I'd meet with parents and say, 'Your child is going to learn, XYZ.' And they would say, 'My child can't do that; she's only three.'"

However, Celeste fulfilled their promises. "By the middle of the school year, their child was writing their first and last name, they were reading a bit, and they were doing math. And parents were like, 'You weren't kidding.'"

How did she consistently achieve these results? First, she made sure that every child felt welcome. "I'd always tell the parents, 'These are my kids.' I'd hug all the kids and all the parents because they might not have been getting hugs elsewhere," she said. "Every year, I would get phenomenal children in my class, hone their abilities and take them to the next level."

Celeste understands that many parents struggle and may not have been raised with the best role models. In fact, her own childhood was far from easy.

"I've been through some stuff, and that's why I'm like I am. My mother was a substance abuser, and she was an alcoholic. And I said, if I ever had kids, I would not treat them the way my mother treated me."

Growing up in such a stressful household taught Celeste to be resilient, and to trust that she could forge a more promising future by believing in herself.

"She loved me, but my mother was dealing with a lot of stuff. Some of what happened to her also happened to me."

Earlier in her career, Celeste's maternal instincts motivated her to want to raise her own child, but doctors told her she could not give birth. The news was devastating. "I was very depressed," she recalls.

She strongly desired to share her teaching gifts with a child she could mentor for life. By way of a colleague, providence brought her Jason, a 2-month-old child needing fostering. "He is a former coworker's cousin. She took in his brother but didn't have space for him, so I said, I'll take him."

Their bond was immediate. "When I took him to visit my mom, she said, 'That's your baby.' Everybody in my family fell in love with him," Celeste said.

Being a single working mother is rarely easy, but Celeste was prepared to meet the challenge. Accepting Jason as her own, four months later, she successfully petitioned to adopt him. "It was the best decision I ever made," Celeste said.

She focused her energy on Jason's well-being by creating a nurturing environment reliant on open communication. "Every day, I made sure to tell him, 'I love you.'"

"I would ask him, 'Is there anything I can do better as a mother?'" In turn, Jason would ask her, "Is there anything I can do better as a son?"

Despite best intentions, they would have occasional rough patches. "We've had rocky times, but I never disrespected him," she said. "Sometimes, we would have a spat before he would leave for school. But I would still text him, 'I love you, son.' You know, I apologize."

Celeste acknowledges that many parents don't believe it is appropriate to apologize to their children. They may feel it diminishes their authority or makes them appear weak. She strongly disagrees. "Yes, you should because you're not right all the time."

She reinforced these messages with a regular practice. "I'd tell him, you look in the mirror every day and tell yourself that you are destined for greatness. And, tell yourself that you love you." It was simple advice that began to pay off.

Aware of the circumstances and pitfalls that can lead young males of color astray, Celeste ensured that Jason benefited from her early childhood teaching expertise.

"I did everything and am still doing everything to make sure my child doesn't become a statistic."

She paid close attention and supported his curiosities and talents. "Like everything he did. He wrote his first book at age eight, got it published at nine, and had three books published by the time he was ten."

Jason dedicated his first book to President Barack Obama and sent him a copy. The former president returned the sentiment with a personal letter stating, "I know you'll do great things."

Still, Jason faced challenges. At age 7, he was diagnosed with Attention Deficit Hyperactivity Disorder (ADHD), and they discovered he had inherited bipolar disorder.

"I knew he was going to have some challenges because his birth parents had mental health challenges, but we've been able to manage it since kindergarten," Celeste said. "He actually came to me and said, 'What's wrong with me, Mom? I just can't control myself.'"

Working as an educator had benefits. Celeste sought out and bonded with other teachers who became allies at each school Jason attended. "I was blessed to find someone at every school to watch out for my baby," she said.

It is the kind of relationship she believes every parent can achieve with their child's teachers. It requires a "takes a village" attitude, fostering the belief that this is not only "my child," but also "our child." It is what's possible when parents and teachers work together to ensure a child's growth and well-being.

Celeste discovered parents could secure assistance from an *educational advocate*, especially if their child has special needs. She recommends using Google and the search term: "educational advocate near me" to find local support. Unlike attorneys, these professionals are trained to advise parents about their rights and intervene when necessary.

She also encouraged Jason to reframe his thinking about his diagnosis. "Don't let it hinder you," she would say. "Use it as your superpower. It's not a disability; it's an 'other' ability."

Jason is now a graduating junior, finishing a year early and preparing for his first year of college. He dreams of becoming a sports broadcast analyst and perhaps one day working for ESPN.

The takeaways from Celeste and Jason's story are significant. First, she saw promise in every child, regardless of background, never viewing challenging circumstances as deficits. She consistently reinforced the message, "You are loved, whole, and complete," regardless of diagnoses or socioeconomic setbacks.

She had high expectations for her students and son, seeing greatness in them that they might not yet see themselves. And she reinforced these sentiments daily.

Additionally, Celeste cultivated a collaborative relationship with Jason's teachers and their colleagues to surround him with a supportive network. They pledged to maintain a watchful eye to ensure he stayed on course.

We don't choose the circumstances or domestic settings that shape our destiny. However, setbacks need not predict our future. Challenged by misfortune, it wasn't easy for Celeste's mother to give her a similar level of positive nurturing. Yet, an underlying sense of her mother's love guided Celeste to thrive and give that gift to her students and her child.

Not every child will emerge to author a book by age 8 or correspond with a U.S. President. However, their example demonstrates what's possible when we honor a child's intrinsic interests and cheer them on.

It's also important to acknowledge that not every parent has a network of educators or a disposable income that affords unique experiences. However, we should never overlook the fact that encouraging a child's interests can begin with a library book. There are free virtual experiences designed for kids. Also, often, you can secure scholarships for specialized camps and internships.

Benefits come from listening, observing, and open communication. Listen and observe your child's genuine curiosities, and nurture those interests. This is also how we cultivate character in children. Communicate openly, and build a relationship based on mutual respect and trust.

KEY TAKEAWAYS

This chapter primarily shared the story of an early childhood educator who developed successful strategies that benefited students beyond their parents' expectations. She longed to give her gifts to a child of her own. After discovering she could not give birth, she adopted and mentored a son who has flourished from her approach. She shares candidly about how parents can follow her lead.

QUESTIONS TO CONSIDER

- How might you reinforce the message that the young people in your life are "loved, whole, and complete"?
- What are their curiosities and how might you support them?
- How might you tap into a support network that is aligned with your commitments?

Chapter 10

Call to Action

Politicians promise to transform and improve our public education system in each election cycle. However, time and time again, they have failed to deliver on these promises. Instead, their policies have often resulted in unintended consequences and further perpetuated inequality in the education system. We need to look no further than the No Child Left Behind Act, which was signed into law by President George W. Bush in 2002. The law aimed to hold schools accountable for student performance by requiring annual standardized testing and imposing penalties for schools that failed to meet performance standards. However, the law had the unintended consequence of narrowing the curriculum and placing too much emphasis on test scores, which led to a decline in student engagement and critical thinking skills (Klien, 2023).

Another example is the push for charter schools and school vouchers, which elected officials have championed as a way to increase school choice and improve academic outcomes. However, studies have shown that charter schools often perform no better than traditional public schools and the proliferation of charter schools has led to increased segregation and inequality in some communities (Valent, 2020).

More recently, the COVID-19 pandemic has highlighted politicians' failures to address the education system's systemic issues. The shift to remote learning has exacerbated existing inequalities, with students from low-income families and marginalized communities facing greater barriers to accessing education. Many politicians have failed to take meaningful action despite calls for increased funding and resources to address these issues.

Under-resourced schools face significant challenges that make it difficult to provide a high-quality education to their students. These schools typically lack the necessary funding, staffing, and resources to meet the needs of their students, particularly those who come from low-income families or have learning disabilities.

These schools often lack funding, leading to a lack of essential resources, such as textbooks, technology, and classroom materials. In some cases, schools may not have enough funding to hire a sufficient number of teachers or support staff to meet the needs of their students. This can lead to a high turnover rate, which can be disruptive for students who need stability in their education. It can also result in a lack of experienced teachers with the necessary skills to work with students with learning disabilities or other special needs.

WAITING IS NO LONGER AN OPTION

Education is one of the most important pillars of our society, and ensuring that our children have access to quality education is essential for their success and our country's future. However, the current education system faces numerous challenges, including funding shortages, standardized testing, and issues of inequality and access. As a parent, you are critical in advocating for change and ensuring that your child receives the best possible education.

Examples of successful parental advocacy in education are evident throughout our nation's history. In 1963, a group of African American parents in Chicago decided to take action against the poor quality of education and segregation in their schools. They organized a boycott of the Chicago Public Schools (CPS) that lasted several days and gained national attention.

Led by civil rights activist and minister Reverend Jesse Jackson, the boycott addressed Chicago's poverty, discrimination, and inequality. An estimated 200,000 students stayed home from school during the three-day protest. Parents and activists demanded an end to overcrowded classrooms, inadequate facilities, and unequal treatment of African American students. They also called for the resignation of the district's superintendent (Dickson, 2013).

The protest received national attention and pressured the city and state to address the issues the parents and activists raised. As a result, several changes were made to the education system in Chicago, including the creation of local school councils and the desegregation of schools. The boycott inspired similar protests in other cities, including New York and Detroit.

Another example is the New York City Coalition for Educational Justice (CEJ), a grassroots organization formed in 2010 in response to the growing disparities in the New York City education system. The coalition comprises parents, students, educators, and community organizers committed to ensuring that all students in New York City have access to quality education.

CEJ has successfully advocated for systemic changes in the education system in New York City. One of their major accomplishments was securing increased funding for underfunded schools in the city. The coalition worked with city officials and policymakers to advocate for a more equitable funding formula to ensure that all schools in the city received adequate resources and support.

The organization has also been instrumental in advocating for changes in education policy in New York City. They have pushed for policies that prioritize the needs of students and that ensure access to quality education. Some of their successes include advocating for changes to the school discipline code to reduce the number of suspensions and expulsions and advocating for implementing restorative justice practices in schools.

One of the most significant accomplishments of CEJ was its successful advocacy for changes to the admissions process for New York City's specialized high schools. These schools had historically relied on a single test to determine admissions, which had led to a lack of diversity in the student body. CEJ worked with community groups and city officials to advocate for a more holistic admissions process that considers factors such as grades, attendance, and extracurricular activities.

Through its advocacy efforts, CEJ has brought attention to the issues facing students in New York City and pushed for meaningful change in the education system. Their work serves as a model for other parent-led organizations and demonstrates the power of collective action in making a difference in students' lives.

PARENT ADVOCACY INTO ACTION

As a parent, you have the power to make a difference in your child's education. Your involvement and advocacy can significantly impact their academic success and the quality of education they receive. It's time to take action and fight for your child's future.

First and foremost, you need to understand your child's individual needs and challenges. This means taking the time to communicate with their teachers and school administrators and understanding their strengths and weaknesses. With this knowledge, you can begin to advocate for the support and resources your child needs to succeed.

Remember, you are not alone in this fight. Many advocacy groups and organizations are working to improve education for all children, and you can join them in their efforts. Collaborating with other parents and advocates can build a strong network and a united front focused on creating positive change.

Effective advocacy requires clear and effective communication. You must clearly articulate your concerns and goals and work collaboratively with school administrators and policymakers to achieve them. This may involve attending meetings, writing letters, or organizing and participating in community events.

Finally, it's important to remember that change takes time and perseverance. You may face obstacles and setbacks, but don't give up. Your advocacy efforts can significantly impact your child's education and the education of all children in your community.

In conclusion, as a parent, you can make a difference in your child's education. By understanding their needs, collaborating with other parents and advocates, communicating effectively, and persevering in your efforts, you can impact their academic success and the quality of education they receive. It's time to take action and fight for your child's future.

INSPIRING STUDENT ADVOCATES

As parents, one of our most important jobs is preparing our children for world success. While we often focus on teaching them academic skills and good behavior, self-advocacy is another important life skill.

Teaching your child to advocate for themselves means giving them the tools and confidence they need to speak up for their own needs and goals. This critical skill will serve them well throughout their lives, helping them navigate challenges, pursue their dreams, and stand up for what they believe in.

By teaching your child to advocate for themselves, you are helping them to develop a strong sense of self-worth and independence. They will learn to trust their judgment and confidently voice their opinions, enabling them to make better decisions and be more successful in school, work, and relationships.

Self-advocacy is also an essential skill for navigating the challenges of the modern world. With so much noise and distraction, getting what you need and achieving your goals can be difficult. By teaching your child to advocate for themselves, you are giving them the tools to cut through the noise and make their voices heard.

Most importantly, teaching your child to advocate for themselves sends a powerful message: they are capable, strong, and worthy of respect. It shows them they can shape their own lives and make a difference in the world.

In conclusion, teaching your child to advocate for themselves is one of the most important gifts you can give them. It will help them to develop a strong sense of self-worth, independence, and confidence and enable them to achieve their goals and make a difference in the world. So don't wait—start teaching your child to advocate for themselves today.

At the Journalistic Learning Initiative, we're committed to bringing about a global shift in how to engage students and advance education. Our philosophy privileges project-based storytelling, which honors students' passion and promise. For more information, visit: http://journalisticlearning.org.

KEY TAKEAWAYS

This chapter stressed that committed action is crucial for enacting meaningful change. It cited examples of inspiring grassroots coalitions that have achieved significant results. More so, it reinforced the importance of empowering young people to advocate for themselves. It's the key to developing their curiosity, confidence, and character.

QUESTIONS TO CONSIDER

- What small first step might you take today toward a more significant vision to make a difference in educational experiences?
- Where might you find like-minded allies?
- In what ways can you empower young people to advocate for themselves?

REFERENCES

Dickson, R. (2013, October 22). *1963 Chicago Public School Boycott*. WTTW News. Retrieved April 12, 2023, from https://news.wttw.com/2013/10/22/1963-chicago-public-school-boycott

Klein, A. (2023, March 24). No child left behind: An overview. *Education Week*. Retrieved April 12, 2023, from https://www.edweek.org/policy-politics/no-child-left-behind-an-overview/2015/04

Valant, J. (2020, October 1). *What are charter schools and do they deliver?* Brookings. Retrieved April 12, 2023, from https://www.brookings.edu/policy2020/votervital/what-are-charter-schools-and-do-they-deliver/

Appendix

List of *Parent Advocacy Resources*

1. National Parent Teacher Association (PTA)—www.pta.org
2. National Center for Learning Disabilities—www.ncld.org
3. Council for Exceptional Children—www.cec.sped.org
4. National Alliance on Mental Illness (NAMI)—www.nami.org
5. American Speech-Language-Hearing Association (ASHA)—www.asha.org
6. Understood.org—www.understood.org
7. Disability Rights Education and Defense Fund—www.dredf.org
8. The Advocacy Institute—www.advocacyinstitute.org
9. National Down Syndrome Society—www.ndss.org
10. Autism Speaks—www.autismspeaks.org
11. The Arc—www.thearc.org
12. National Association of Parents with Children in Special Education (NAPCSE)—www.napcse.org
13. Special Education Advocacy and Law Firm (SEAL)—www.specialedadvocacy.org
14. Wrightslaw—www.wrightslaw.com
15. Parent Advocacy Coalition for Educational Rights (PACER)—www.pacer.org
16. National Federation of the Blind (NFB)—www.nfb.org
17. The Dyslexia Resource—www.dyslexiaresource.org
18. The Tourette Association of America—www.tourette.org
19. CHADD (Children and Adults with Attention-Deficit/Hyperactivity Disorder)—www.chadd.org

20. International Dyslexia Association—www.dyslexiaida.org
21. Learning Disabilities Association of America (LDA)—www.ldaamerica.org
22. National Center for Educational Statistics (NCES)—nces.ed.gov
23. National Dissemination Center for Children with Disabilities (NICHCY)—nichcy.org
24. National Organization for Rare Disorders (NORD)—rarediseases.org
25. Parents, Let's Unite for Kids (PLUK)—pluk.org
26. National Association of School Psychologists (NASP)—nasponline.org
27. National Council of Teachers of Mathematics (NCTM)—nctm.org
28. National Science Teachers Association (NSTA)—nsta.org
29. National Association of Music Merchants Foundation (NAMM)—nammfoundation.org
30. National Art Education Association (NAEA)—arteducators.org
31. Association for Middle Level Education (AMLE)—amle.org
32. National Association for Gifted Children (NAGC)—nagc.org
33. National Association of Secondary School Principals (NASSP)—nassp.org
34. National Association of Elementary School Principals (NAESP)—naesp.org
35. National Association of School Nurses (NASN)—nasn.org
36. National Parent Leadership Institute (NPLI)—parentleaders.org
37. National Center on Accessible Educational Materials (AEM Center)—aem.cast.org
38. National Dropout Prevention Center/Network (NDPC/N)—dropoutprevention.org
39. National High School Center (NHSC)—schoollabs.com/national-high-school-center
40. National Youth Leadership Network (NYLN)—nyln.org
41. Center for Parent Information and Resources (CPIR)—parentcenterhub.org
42. National Center for Education Research and Technology (NCERT)—ncerthelp.org
43. National Education Association (NEA)—nea.org
44. Institute for Literacy (NIFL)—nifl.gov
45. National Science Foundation (NSF)—nsf.gov

46. National Council for the Social Studies (NCSS)—socialstudies.org
47. National Association of Independent Schools (NAIS)—nais.org
48. National Association of School Superintendents (NASS)—nass.us
49. National Education Association Foundation (NEAF)—neafoundation.org
50. National Center for Learning Disabilities—www.ncld.org

www.ingramcontent.com/pod-product-compliance
Lightning Source LLC
Chambersburg PA
CBHW030146240426
43672CB00005B/292